POLITICAL ORDER AND T

POLITICAL ORDER AND THE LAW OF LABOUR

Geoffrey Kay and James Mott

First published 1982 by
THE MACMILLAN PRESS LTD
London and Basingstoke
Companies and representatives
throughout the world

Hardcover ISBN 0 333 27152 1
Paperback ISBN 0 333 27154 8

Printed in Hong Kong

To Ulrich, the man without qualities

Contents

Preface

Imagine – in a night of mysterious events all the screwdrivers in the world disappeared, and all memory of them as well, so that in the morning nobody knew what a screwdriver was, or whether, for that matter, there had ever been such a thing. But if screwdrivers alone had vanished and everything else remained, there would be an urgent need to re-invent them. Now let us stretch our imagination further and suppose that social scientists were charged with this task, and were organised into two teams – the traditionalists and the modernists. Both teams would face the same problem and both would have the same materials to hand – billions of screws of all sizes, shapes and tensions, performing myriad functions. The traditionalists, guided by Machiavelli, Hobbes, Rousseau, Kant, Smith, Ricardo, Hegel, Marx and Lenin, would know that this complexity of effects must have a simple cause, and rapidly solve the problem. The modernists, mostly French and inspired by Bachelard to have no fear of complexity, would invent a grotesque armature with numerous over-determined blades articulated through a structure that specified their relative autonomy. Their English followers would make a plastic copy and then, disenchanted, pour scorn on the whole project and claim there was no such thing as a screwdriver, and to think otherwise was epistemologically unsound.

We thank Mary Keane for her care in typing.

The City University, London   GEOFFREY KAY
August 1981   JAMES MOTT

1 Absolute Property

In modern society, where the conditions of life are private property, needs are separated from capacities. A state of abundance would alter this. Needs and capacities would come together, and close off the space between them. In modern society, this space is filled by the dense structures of private property – political order and the law of labour: in a state of abundance they would have no place. If the productive capacities already deployed were oriented towards need, necessary labour would be reduced to a minimum, so that nothing would stand between men and what they need to live. Money and the law of labour would lose their force, and, as its foundations crumbled, the political state would wither away. The state of abundance is not a Utopian vision but the real possibility of conditions already in existence. As the twentieth-century version of the 'state of nature' originally invented by political philosophy as modern society was taking shape, abundance keeps the tradition of criticism alive.

The great tradition of political philosophy from the sixteenth to the eighteenth century realised that private property and contract lay at the heart of political society. It contrasted the world to a conjectured epoch from which it was believed to have originated. Viewing political society in the light of its past, as opposed to its future, philosophy resorted to atavism and gave prominence to a natural state or human condition. In this state of nature, the right to property was present, but unable to establish an order capable of ensuring its survival. Hence the need for its formalisation into a political state. But while private property could be extrapolated back into the state of nature, it is not possible to reverse the procedure, and project it forward to a state of abundance. Rousseau said men were forced to quit the natural state because their powers as persons become inadequate to sustain them: but he did not envisage the immense development of productive forces that began with the industrial revolution. The development of human capacities to become embodied in self-regulating machines, points to the possibility of furnishing the needs of subsistence with a minimum of living labour. This confirms the conclusion of natural law, that private property is at the heart of political society, only the emphasis is altered. Where political philosophy believed private property was fundamental, and accepted the state as its guarantee, the theory of abundance sees private property as a phase in the development of social production, which the state now protects simply to preserve its own existence. As the growth of productive powers threatens private property, the state is forced to an evermore frenzied organisation of its defence. The simple truth of political society is that it rests upon private property: this was firmly grasped by philosophers of the state of nature, but they did not see beyond it.

At the heart of its theory of private property, natural law placed labour – man's relation to nature, posed in terms of legal persons and things. This gave rise to the elementary form of private property, *persona-res*. But contrary to first impressions this elementary form of property is not a self-contained structure of a person and a thing. It is a social order within which each act of ownership is general in so far as it must ban trespass. But though private property always takes the form of a social relation among persons, it is not one in which things play a passive role. In political society things have a life of their own.

In the eighteenth century, man was not conceived apart from nature; on the contrary, he was its most vital part, since it was through man that nature became conscious of itself. A central category of philosophy at that time was reason, which as the unified order of persons and things was both natural and human. Each individual was capable of participating in reason and providing himself with adequate materials of knowledge. But at the same time as they celebrated this unified order, philosophers became aware that it was being torn apart by private property and the division of labour. The formation of the proletariat in the late eighteenth century as a class of men completely cut off from the conditions of life (i.e. nature) brought this philosophic project of unified order to an end. After 1848 the philosophy of universal harmony split into the apologetics for the existing order and revolutionary opposition to it.

PRIVATE PROPERTY

Where private property is the universal mode of appropriation, the legal form *persona-res* is the sinew that binds society together. The need for such a specially developed bond only arises when the elements linked by it are denied the possibility of establishing a direct unity in themselves. The very existence of a legal bond between persons and things presupposes their real separation. In fact, private property presupposes not just one but a whole series of separations of which this is the first: namely, the material conditions of life are legal things over which no person can exercise a direct claim. Nothing in capitalist society can be acquired through simple possession or natural right, since there are no direct relations between men and the world about them. Thus the first separation implied by private property as a condition of its existence, and a condition continually reproduced by its existence, is a categorical split between persons and things, which far from being overcome by their refinement into legal subjects and objects, is reinforced by it. This primary separation is complemented by a second – the division of subject from subject and object from object – through which property is made to work as a system.

The distinctive feature of modern property that sets it apart from the earlier and less developed forms of classical antiquity and feudalism, is that these two separations, which result in a world of individual subjects on the one side and discrete objects on the other, have become absolute by combining to form a third: the separation of the right to property from all objects. In capitalist society the legal capacities that stamp an individual as an owner of property are not derived from direct possession. Where property is absolute in this sense (*absolute property*) a wedge is driven between the right of ownership and all objects, creating a gulf between subjects and objects and opening a space which is immediately filled by the state. The sequence is logical, not temporal: the separation of subjectivity from objects does not happen first in time creating a space that the state subsequently occupies, the events occur simultaneously. The space is filled at the very moment of its creation, since it is in the nature of this space that it can only exist as occupied space. The founding of absolute property and the establishment of the state are reciprocal moments of the same process.

It is convenient to follow the route taken by natural law since its simple experiments give quick access to private property. Consider the situation where individuals meet irregularly to trade their wares. Every act of exchange requires its parties to recognise each other as property owners, but where exchange is irregular the recognition is specific as regards time, place, parties and goods. *A* needs to recognise the property rights of *B* only on the occasion of their barter, and then only in respect to the particular object he seeks to acquire from him: *B*'s recognition of *A* is similarly restricted. But in capitalist society where exchange is general and impersonal, the right to property cannot be established in such a piecemeal way. In fact it is established independently of all and any specifics of time, place, parties and goods. Where trade proceeds irregularly, individuals establish their property rights through acts of exchange: in capitalist society they are fully established as property owners before they enter the market, and the right to property is unlimited. In this sense the subjectivity of the individual as a person with the legal capacity to own property, is universal. *Universal subjectivity*: (1) it is not restricted to particular objects and occasions; (2) it applies to all individuals. As bearers of this universal subjectivity, members of society lose all marks of distinction and move on the same plane as equivalents.

Universal subjectivity came into being only when productive forces and the division of labour achieved a definite level of development, but even then it did not arise spontaneously. Thus private property has developed through a mass of laws which express its conditions and its operations; and the legal formula *persona-res* has always been embodied in a large number of detailed laws of contract, tort, theft, trespass and so on. It was through these laws that modern subjectivity arose and through their elaboration that it developed towards universality. But it would be wrong to read the state into this process as a constant or given factor, since this would deny its historical character. The legislation that founded modern property transformed men and their real conditions of subsistence into subjects and objects of property. And *at the same time transformed the law-making body into the political state*. The first acts of modern property were effected through the offices of the feudal suzerain, which in the process assumed the depersonalised character of a monarchy. This was then set at a distance from the other feudal orders and opened the way for the new political division of the state from civil society. The modern law of property was not entirely new at its inception, but depended heavily upon Roman law which had already developed the concepts of legal personality and public sovereignty, though not to the full and absolute extent they were to achieve in capitalist society. The transformation of feudal orders through the medium of Roman law took centuries; the outcome was never inevitable and like all actual history it pursued an uncertain and wavering course. Yet its process was determined at every moment by the connection of private property to the state without which not only the past but also the present would be a senseless chaos.

The logical structure of absolute property comprises three elements:

(1) subjects are pulled away from objects in so far as subjectivity is not defined in relation to any particular object;
(2) subjects approach objects through an already established universal right of ownership applicable to any object;
(3) all elements of the natural world are defined as objects in as much as all of them qualify for appropriation by subjects.

It is a structure that presupposes the existence of a state for it is only through the medium of a state that persons and things can be formally constituted as subjects and objects prior to their actual collisions. On the other side, it is equally certain that political authority in society only assumes the form of a state where real appropriation is effected through legal subjects and objects that are constituted prior to it.

The direct encounter of a subject with an object spells the destruction of the object, for it is the act of consumption. Thus the property relation only really flourishes in the moment between production and consumption when the object moves in the sphere of circulation and is exchanged as a commodity. The act of exchange which moves the commodity into the sphere of consumption is a bilateral relation between subjects in which they accord each other recognition. Two independent wills meet and recognise themselves in each other. So complete is reciprocity in this act, and the consequent identity of the parties involved, that classical German philosophy conceived the prime mover at work here as a common or universal will that transcended the individuals actually involved, who merely participated in it. The idealist character of this conception can easily be criticised, particularly the notion that universal will had origins outside the actual practice of exchange; but this does not diminish the achievement of German philosophy in recognising that exchange was more than a series of collisions and a determinate structure from the very outset. Where natural law took as its starting-point random exchanges that had to be harmonised and stabilised, German philosophy proposed that it came into the world fully formed. For this reason it could not grasp the real history of exchange: however, it brought to the fore the fact that exchange in modern society is not a self-sufficient system but one which presupposes a constitutive force.

Both natural law and German classical philosophy in their different ways grasped the fact that private property could only become the general form of appropriation (absolute property) on condition of the existence of the state. Both traditions understood that exchange takes place on terms that are established outside its immediate sphere. On the side of objectivity so much is explicit in the fact that modern exchange is transacted through a universal object (money), which though it originates in exchange as an object like all others, only begins to develop its universality when it stands apart and becomes a political object. The political nature of money is evident in its appearance – it always bears the head of the prince, or some other emblem of state. On the side of subjectivity the same applies: just as money is immediately exchangeable as a universal object whose credentials do not have to be checked, so every individual is accepted at face value as a *persona bona fide*. Money is accepted because it is a universal object on account of its being political: the individual is universally recognised because he is a political subject – a citizen.

In everyday affairs the matter is taken for granted: in more substantial transactions such as the sale and purchase of a house, searches are made into title; but these searches are restricted to the claim of the seller to be the owner, and do not extend to his legal capacity to own the house in the first place. A legal curiosity is that the searches have to establish that the house is indeed an object of property that can be alienated absolutely, since houses are a sub-category of what was previously known as real property, and in some cases medieval rights of usage still attach. But this anomaly of real property, where feudal forms linger on and leave their traces in modern society, is precisely the exception that proves the rule; that in political society all persons and things, by virtue of being in political society under the state, exist immediately as subjects and objects of property. While theorists of natural law understood this well, that absolute property could only exist within the framework of the political state, the relation has to be reversed to show that the structures of power take the form of the state because private property rules absolutely. The reason for this is the possibility of a state of abundance.

Since social relations in political society are conducted on grounds of reciprocity, they cannot have political content as they did in feudal society. Hence it follows that the locus of power and authority in political society must be thrust outside the sphere of social relations and stand apart from it as a sovereign, giving rise to the division of the state from civil society that took shape in the sixteenth, seventeenth and eighteenth centuries. It is the hallmark of the state that it stands apart from society and exercises power over it from a distance. And it is this very distance from society, which on the one hand makes it universal (i.e. the same for all members of society), and on the other allows it to impose universality back upon society. Liberal theory has conflated this universality with an all-encompassing dogmatic theory of democracy.

INTENSIFIED PROPERTY

The theory of a state of nature survived into the eighteenth century when it was still reasonable to imagine that private property was natural. A philosopher could peer through the legal categories of subject and object and still see men and nature through them, although Rousseau and Kant found this increasingly difficult. In the nineteenth century with the intensification of property this could no longer be done rationally, since anyone who looked closely at either of the elements of intensified property merely saw an inverted image of the other. Close examination of capital revealed labour-power, while detailed inspection of labour-power pointed to capital. Political economy which continued the tradition of natural law, thought that when it peered at labour and capital it could see nature, but this illusion was no longer reasonable. The contribution to political philosophy by the theory of a state of nature was the political division of the state from civil society. This arose from absolute property and at the same time established it as a series of separations: (1) subject from object; (2) subject from subject; (3) object from object; resumed in the separation of (4) subjectivity from all objects (universal subjectivity). These separations were limited by the unity from which they were derived: namely, a direct relation between man and his surroundings in a state of nature. Eighteenth-century rationalism appreciated these separations as artificial, but by contrasting them to a conjectured unity, it became unable to apprehend the real nature of the tensions involved in them, and therefore their limits, and the limits of political society. The theory of abstraction which substitutes the state of abundance for that of nature elaborates these selfsame separations but in revolutionary terms that reveal these limits.

When private property is absolute, not only do all subjects of property become equivalent to each other and all objects likewise uniform, but subjects and objects are merged into each other in an entirely new way. The new equivalence of absolute property encompasses both subjects and objects in its formal order, and it is this which makes possible the intensification of property into capital and labour-power. Subjectivity and objectivity, in the legal form *persona-res*, remain the model of property intensified in this way.

The commodities consumed as the physical elements of capital (machines, raw materials), and the money advanced for their purchase, are commodities like all others: but when they serve as capital they undergo a change that sets them apart. A corresponding metamorphosis occurs in their legal form, and capital-as-property is as distinct from simple property as commodity-capital is from the simple commodity. After the latter is purchased it is at the disposal of its owner to use as he pleases, but this can never be the case with capital. Capital is value-in-motion; commodities bought and sold, repurchased and resold, for profit (surplus value) and not personal consumption. Furthermore profit is independent of the will of the owner, in that it arises directly from the activity of buying in order to sell. The process of accumulation does not originate in the appetites of capitalists and can even move against them. If an individual capitalist exercises his formal option of consuming his capital rather than re-advancing it in search of profit, he ceases *ipso facto* to be a capitalist. But even a more limited exercise of his will against accumulation, such as the personal consumption of a part of profits, is subject to constraint. Property only functions as capital when it is continually re-advanced in search of profit, and the individual capitalist can only remain in business by accepting the external discipline of the market and investing enough to keep abreast of new techniques and efficient organisation. The same restrictions apply to the whole class of capitalists. The pace and pattern of accumulation is determined by *capital-in-general*, which is not a simple aggregation of individual capitals but their totality. This totality is not formed by a conscious coalition of individual capitalists; on the contrary it operates through their mutual antipathy (competition). The subject of capital-in-general is the capitalist class, but since capital is exercised as private property this subject is decomposed and inadequate to its object. The resulting mismatch of subject and object provides the opportunity for a revolution whereby the latter seizes the initiative. The hallmark of private property as capital is precisely this dispossession of the subject's will.

The general circuit of capital, $M-C-M'$ (where M represents money and C a commodity), buying in order to sell, is an inversion of the simple circulation of commodities, $C-M-C'$. The latter represents the exchange of use-values for consumption and keeps the personal subject to the foreground and things in their place as objects of disposition. The former, however, starting and ending with money, so that its only possible end is quantitative gain – an excess of M' over M or surplus value – brings the object to the fore where it is in a position to dispose of the subject. An individual may choose to become a capitalist, but having made this choice the logic of accumulation disposes of his will. At the same time even the possibility of this choice presupposes property in excess of personal requirements and, in this respect, already prefigures the nature of capital as property apart from any needs of the subject. In the circuit of capital, commodities as use-values become a means of circulating values; while money, the universal commodity that is indifferent to particular use-values and hence indifferent to needs, closes the circle with itself and takes itself as its own criterion. The separation of subject from object that lies at the heart of simple property is intensified as the object declares its independence.

For this reason the classic legal form of property, *persona-res*, is quite inadequate for capital. Just as capital is its own criterion, and accumulation an end in itself, so the legal form of capital discards all external subjects. The establishment of this legal form in the nineteenth century, the joint stock company with limited liability, is often interpreted as an *ad hoc* measure to protect the interests of individual investors, but this fails to grasp its real significance. While legislation was occasioned by specific circumstances, it is important to understand that the need for a special legal subjectivity for capital arises from the nature of capital as such, and that the circumstances that made such legislation imperative, and the form this legislation assumed when it was finally passed, have much deeper causes than frauds in the 1860s.

The feature of nineteenth-century legislation still crucial today, despite the elaborate growth of corporate law, is the limitation of the liability of any individual investor to the amount of his investment. This separates the personal property of the individual from his capital, and thus gives legal recognition to the real differences between them. But at the same time as investors are relieved of liability beyond their capital, they are also spared the liabilities of this capital, in that such claims as arise through its employment are directed against the company or corporation and not the shareholders. In other words, the institution of limited liability established the corporation as a new and independent legal subject every bit as real in law as the personal subjects of the classic legal form, though totally removed from these subjects. The corporation is the real or active owner of the capital it employs: where this capital is the object of property, the corporation is the subject. On the other hand, the corporation comprises nothing but capital – the investments of shareholders: so that capital is present at both poles of property, as both subject and object. This is the characteristic legal form of capital corresponding adequately to its economic form. Just as money which is indifferent to commodities as use-values and hence indifferent to need, becomes both premise and result of the economic circuit of capital, so the subject and object of capital-as-property acquire a unity which is similarly indifferent to conditions outside itself.

The intensification of property into industrial capital requires the transformation of the capacity to labour into a commodity and results in a legal form which is the antithesis to that of capital. Whereas with capital the object of property becomes subject; with labour the movement takes place in the opposite direction, as the subject comes to take itself as object. The worker sells his labour-power: this presupposes him to be a subject of property which he can legally alienate in the market; and his labour-power, an object of property. But labour-power is not an object in the conventional sense; certainly not one of the type envisaged in natural law. It is not a thing outside the person, but his own capacities or life-force. Since the potential locked up in this capacity, labour, can only be realised through the worker himself, it follows that the object of which the worker is subject is nothing but himself.

This is the antithesis of labour and capital: in one case the object of property becomes its own subject; in the other the subject becomes object. But these opposed forms of intensified property are made up of identical elements. Both capital and labour are made out of the subjects and objects of the elementary legal form of private property; and the fact that they have this in common is a feature of their antithesis. It is only in capitalist society that

uniformity exists as the medium through which opposed classes can
take each other as equivalents. In the buying and selling of labour-
power (wage labour) the two intensified forms of property meet
directly. But this meeting has the nature of a contradiction because
it brings together common elements structured in entirely opposed
ways. On both sides there are subjects and objects, but in reverse
order. It is only because they are composed of identical elements
that capital and labour-power are able to meet at all; the reverse
ordering of these elements dictates that this meeting is a
contradiction.

This contradiction can be perceived within the structure of the
wage itself, whose form is equivalence but whose real content is
exploitation. Formally workers and capital meet as equivalents: as
the legal subjects of property they seek to exchange labour-power on
the one side and money on the other. But the real contents of the
exchange are not equivalent since the worker, in agreeing to sell his
labour-power, agrees in effect to submit his will to its purchaser, and
work under stipulated conditions. In classical antiquity the slave
was an object of property; in feudal society, the subordination of the
serf was explicit in his status: it is only in capitalist society that social
relations cease to express their real content and obliterate all traces
of exploitation through their organisation as transactions among
equivalents.

Since it is an attribute of the subject, labour-power, like the real
property of feudalism, can never be finally alienated, and is
therefore sold on a periodic basis. This leaves the worker in ultimate
possession of it; hence ultimate possession of himself. The irony of
capitalist society is that the worker is only in full possession of himself
when he is unemployed. Men do not sell their labour-power
naturally, and the political state is necessary before they do so as a
routine that appears natural. The seller of labour-power must be a
free individual endowed with the capacity to own property; and at
the same time a person who has no actual property, since no one
with any independent means of living would sell his labour-power
on a regular and interminable basis. Thus the worker must be at
once a person of property, but a person without property; a subject
of property, but one with no object except his own person. In other
words, the conditions necessary for labour-power to take its place
regularly on the market as a commodity are precisely those that
define universal subjectivity – the right to own property totally
separated from all particular objects of property; hence totally

separated from all real property – *absolute poverty*. The formal content of universal subjectivity is freedom; its real content is the poverty of the proletariat. Absolute property intensified in capitalist society is absolute poverty: the proletarian is the paradigmatic citizen of the political state.

The universal subject is separated from all items of property save one – himself. The only thing to which a citizen can lay direct claim is his own person, and from this property relation (the self owning the self) spring all the rights of modern democracy: the right to strike; free speech and association; due process of law; and the franchise. In the last analysis the structure of right is nothing but the possession of self; liberal democracy nothing but an elaboration of this elemental property form, where the self is thrown back into its self, into loneliness and isolation – *melancholy* (Rousseau); *unhappy consciousness* (Hegel); *social misery* (Marx).

ABSTRACTION AND THE CRITIQUE OF NATURE

In Britain towards the end of the sixteenth century a legal distinction was drawn between the person of the monarch (Elizabeth Tudor or James Stuart) and the monarch as such. Through a doctrine known as the 'king's two bodies' the king was perceived as a *corporation sole*, whereby in addition to a natural person he was recognised as one of a body of monarchs existing through time – the succession:

> . . . the King has in him two Bodies, viz, a Body natural and a Body politic. His Body natural (if it be considered in itself) is a Body mortal, subject to all Infirmities that come by Nature or Accident, to the imbecility of Infancy or Old Age, and the like Defects that happen to the natural Bodies of other People. But his Body politic is a body that cannot be seen or handled, consisting of Policy and Government, and constituted for the Direction of the People, and the Management of the Public Weal, and this Body is utterly void of Infancy and Old Age, and other natural Defects and Imbecilities, which the Body natural is subject to, and for this Cause, what the King does in his Body politic, cannot be invalidated or frustrated by any disability of his Body natural.[1]

Historically an enormous gulf divides the 'Tudor Revolution in

Government' from the consolidation and building of the liberal state in the nineteenth century. Nevertheless this doctrine, formulated at the time when the political state was emerging out of the feudal orders, foreshadows later developments and indicates some of their most essential qualities in a highly graphic way.

The legal division of the king's body is a concrete historical instance of separation associated with private property: the terms of its formulation, which counterpose politics to nature, are those of natural law. For all these reasons: that it is historically concrete; that it expresses the fundamental tenets of natural law in clear and simple terms; and that it directly concerns the formation of the state (sovereignty); this doctrine provides a convenient link between the analysis of property in terms of natural law and its refinement through the concept of abstraction.

Because power in the sixteenth century was conceived as the personal capacity of the monarch, the definition of a man as a social person, apart from, and independent of, his 'natural' being, was restricted to the king. It is only with the development of liberal democracy that it has been broadened to the whole of society; though this has happened remarkably recently. Thus while it is possible to see the kernel of liberal democracy in the reconceptualisation of the monarch in the sixteenth century, and trace the logical movement from one to another smoothly, the actual movement of history was turbulent and uncertain. The redefinition of the feudal monarch precipitated a train of events outside the concern of the lawyers who formulated the doctrine of the 'king's two bodies'; nor did these events flow from it inevitably. Nevertheless the separation of the office of the monarch from the person of the king was a decisive first step in the building of the state; and its theorisation was a set piece in the philosophy of natural law. From its very beginnings this philosophy was the self-consciousness of the state. In the period up to the French Revolution it provided the framework within which political knowledge was developed. In the succeeding half century political developments forced a theoretical reconstruction that was achieved by classical German philosophy. Then in the nineteenth century, with the consolidation of industrial capitalism and the emergence of the working class as an altogether new force in history, a further realignment of political thinking took place as Marx synthesised the two traditions and moved beyond them with the theory of abstraction.

Abstraction, it must be emphasised from the outset, is a real process and not a mental construction. It would appear that an antipathy exists between the *real* and the *abstract*, and that the proper relation of one to the other is that of opposites, i.e. abstract means unreal. But this is not the case. The separation of subject from object, which is one moment of the process of abstraction, is real enough, and defines the absolute poverty of the working class.

In the doctrine of the 'king's two bodies' a clear line is drawn between nature conceived as original, and politics that is derived. Within its framework politics presents itself as an obvious abstraction for two reasons: first, as something taken out of or separated from an original condition; second, as a negation of this original condition. After the separation has occurred all traces of nature disappear, i.e. 'the Body [politic] is utterly void of Infancy and Old Age'. In modern society the status of being a property owner and a citizen, through which an individual exercises political and social capacities, pays as little heed to his natural characteristics as the 'Body politic' of the king does to his 'Body natural'; and liberal democracy congratulates itself on this point, that it establishes rights independently of all 'natural' differences of race, sex, age and so on. But if citizenship is an abstraction from all the particularities of nature in the sense that it disregards them totally, it must at the same time recognise that such particularities do in fact exist – how can something be positively disregarded without being equally positively recognised? Only that which exists in a definite and tangible way can be set aside. Thus, conceiving the constitution of citizenship as an abstraction in terms of natural law, along the lines of the doctrine of the 'king's two bodies', entails accepting a real or natural individuality from which abstraction takes place. Even this is not enough since this real or natural individuality, whatever it may be, can only exist as a series of tangible specifics, for it is only as such that it can stand opposed to abstraction in its character of uniformity. But if such characteristics are supposed to be natural, then the theory of abstraction is faced with the problem of presupposing something which is unknowable – how men lived outside society, when even the possibility of their ever having done so is open to the most serious doubt. Thus the theory of abstraction in so far as it would appear to imply men fully formed by nature with all the specifics of individuality, falls at the first hurdle since it would seem to require a knowledge that can never be obtained.

It is significant that the doctrine of the 'king's two bodies' restricts the concept of human nature to the physical body, but this offers no way out. Even if the existence of an asocial human biology were conceded – a bigger concession than might appear at first sight – the theory of abstraction could make no substantial step forward by its own criteria. While the king's 'Body politic' and modern citizenship can both be considered as abstractions from a natural biology, so could all historical conditions – serfdom, slavery and so on – and the concept of abstraction, so long as it is tethered to natural law, is incapable of distinguishing among them. In other words, a concept of abstraction formulated against the notion of human essence can have no historical precision. It cannot, therefore, sustain the position central to the theory, that abstraction is unique to modern society since this is the only society in which the conditions of life are appropriated in the form of absolute property.

It was only with the intensification of property in the nineteenth century that the old concept of nature could be jettisoned, and a proper theory of abstraction put in its place.

In the Tudor doctrine nature and politics are conceived in terms of simple difference, as two unconnected aspects of life which have nothing in common and stand outside each other: nature is original; politics derived and abstract. In a theory of abstraction taken directly from the doctrine of the 'king's two bodies' politics is dependent upon nature for the obvious reason that neither a king nor anyone else can have social capacities without a 'Body natural', even though this is totally disregarded in these capacities. What is less clear but no less certain, is that the 'Body natural' is just as dependent upon the 'Body politic'; though admittedly this dependence is of a different order. It is only when a king, or for that matter anyone else, acquires a social definition disregarding all particularities of person, that it becomes possible to conceive these particularities as something apart, and propose human nature as self-contained. The idea of a common human nature only entered thought when feudal orders decomposed and the category of station, which combined into a unity what later became separated as persons and offices, passed away with them. Only in modern society, where social capacities are established through a uniform subjectivity set at a distance from all particularities, does the question of an authentic human nature stand out.

By presenting the distinction between politics and nature as one of simple difference, the doctrine of the 'king's two bodies' is a very crude version of the theory of abstraction. A more adequate account must acknowledge:

(1) Whether original or social, there can be no doubt that particularities exist, and that politics is an abstraction from them in the sense that they are not immediately present in the rights and capacities through which individuals act in society.

(2) On the other hand, these particularities can only exist as something distinct from politics when politics is so defined as to take no account of them. Thus politics, abstracted social capacities, are, so to speak, the blank screen on which particularities are projected. It is only on such a screen that they can appear as something distinct.

(3) Thus the appearance of particularities (nature) as an element of social life, depends as much upon the abstraction of politics as the possibility of politics depends upon the presence of living beings. Nature, for this reason, since it only enters social life when politics is abstracted, is therefore itself dependent upon abstraction and cannot be considered original. Understood as an element of social life that contributes to its shape and development, that complex of elements that fall under the rubric of human nature cannot be treated as an original datum given to society from outside; on the contrary, it must be recognised as a social product that only comes into being when the capacities to act in society are defined abstractly. In short, nature is as much an abstraction as politics.

(4) In which case, politics can no longer be taken as an abstraction from nature even though it disregards all particularities.

(5) Abstraction, as social process, however, must finally rest upon that which is not abstract.

(6) Thus it follows that there must be something other than politics and nature which is not an abstraction, but from which the two derive abstractly. The existence of such a third term relieves the theory of abstraction from the burden of an essential human nature but leaves the awkward question as to exactly what this third term is. It is particularly awkward since the third term has to be as original as the traditional concept of nature, and therefore as vulnerable.

Human nature is elusive and it is difficult to say exactly what it is. Even if it was possible to discover an occasion on which pristine human nature could be examined, the problem would still remain of demonstrating that the discoveries made about it were relevant to society. The third term must originate in society itself.

Abstraction, it must be stressed once again, is a real process. Therefore to talk of the non-abstract as real would not adequately distinguish it. The most appropriate term for non-abstraction is *rationality*. The theory of abstraction therefore has three terms: abstract, rational and real. Both the abstract and the rational are real. The problem is that the rational has no direct or immediate empirical form in modern society.

'Every child', wrote Marx, 'knows that a country that ceased to work, I will not say for a year, but for a few weeks, would die.'[2] *Labour*, conceived as the purposive transformation of natural materials to satisfy human needs, is easy to apprehend as the rational kernel of society. The difficulty is that labour taken this way is not the same as labour as it is actually performed in capitalist society (concrete labour), since this is exercised under conditions of abstraction. In capitalist society the expenditure of labour is determined within a process of production whose first purpose is profit: capacities are redefined towards this end and the satisfaction of needs made incidental. This is explicit in the formal conditions of employment:

(1) The worker has no rights in the product of his labour which is the property of his employer.

(2) He enters the process of production through a transaction that separates him not only from what he produces but also from the capacities he exercises in production: by selling his labour-power he transfers the will to dispose of his own activity to another.

(3) In this transaction (the wage relation) all particularity, need and capacity is disregarded as quality: thus diverse capacities are expressed in a common form as money, where they survive vestigially as differences of quantity. The power of abstraction, however, does not end here: as the process of production becomes more fully capitalist, so the actual expenditure of labour (concrete labour) becomes increasingly determined by profit. This is evident in the following:

(4) In work itself skills and the conditions of labour generally, ranging from technologies to the location of production, are not determined by the particular capacities of labour, but by capital. With capitalism fully developed, production determines the capacities of labour and not vice versa;

(5) Output does not register the needs of labour directly engaged in

its production, or even the needs of workers taken as a whole: it is the property of capital, the object of its will, and can only be used to satisfy needs on condition of meeting the criterion of profit;

(6) For all these reasons labour as it actually exists, concrete labour, cannot be taken as it stands as the rational element in society from which abstraction takes place. Since all labour as it is performed in capitalist society is subject to abstraction both formally, and in detail, it follows that non-abstract, i.e. rational, labour, can have no immediate empirical existence. It is impossible to single out any branch of social labour, however useful its product; or any aspect of labour, however serious its purpose, and designate it rational labour. Nevertheless the rationality of labour impresses its conditions upon society.

Production, although it is for profit, can never totally disregard the needs of producers. Individual firms can produce frivolous novelties, but capital-in-general must ensure the reproduction of the labour force. This imperative impresses the rationality of labour upon production generally, but it can also be discerned in the individual act of labour in so far as this is always purposive, and the process of production presupposes its end. In the state of abundance a real unity would be forged between labour as an individual act and labour as a social act, and needs and capacities would be directly aligned. This direct unity or the potential rationality of labour, is shattered in capitalist society, as individual labour is dissociated from social production and needs separated from capacities. Although profit is ideally substituted for labour as the basis of production, this is mitigated as labour asserts its rationality through the abstracted forms of value. Capitalist society can never substitute abstract for rational labour (i.e. surplus value for needs) but must double labour into generalised effort on the one hand, which is indifferent to its material product, and particular labour on the other which produces determinate products out of determinate materials. Rationality under these conditions, the purposive application of capacities for the satisfaction of needs, is not expelled from capitalist society but submerged into the abstract forms of the commodity and its derivatives. The most significant of these derivatives is the separation of the capacity to labour from its needs, and its creation as a commodity. The counterpoint to rationality in capitalist society is therefore the buying and selling of labour-power as a commodity. On the other side the limit upon this transaction is the rationality of labour and the possibility of abundance.

In formalising rationality, abstraction inevitably sets all particularities to one side. Thus, within the doctrine of the 'king's two bodies', the king's 'Body politic' disregards his 'Body natural'; and citizenship overrides all needs and capacities. The real ground of particularity is the labour process, for it is here, through the social development of productivity, that needs and capacities develop their possibilities and acquire definite shape.

It is through labour that man acts upon the world and by changing it simultaneously changes himself. Moreover, since production is in continuous flux, needs and capacities, i.e. particularities, are not constant: nor, because of the division of labour, are they uniformly distributed across society, making individuals facsimiles of each other. Particularity arising out of labour therefore, unlike human nature seen in essentialist terms, varies along two axes simultaneously: across society and through time.

Concrete labour is fully subsumed by abstraction (capital) both formally and really. Nevertheless the needs and capacities of labour are not constituted exclusively by capital: labour is not conjured up by capital but is an external condition to be taken and formalised. It is in this irreducible character of labour that the third term in the formula of abstraction can be found.

Natural law, as it is expressed in the doctrine of the 'king's two bodies', counterposes politics (explicit abstraction) to nature (particularity) as though the latter in its existing empirical form is not already determined by abstraction. It treats politics and nature in terms of simple difference, as though they were independent of each other and capable of standing alone. But since both are determined by abstraction this approach rests upon a false premise. Hence its conclusion that politics is the abstraction of society; a superstructure that rests upon a non-abstract base, actually existing nature or economics, as it came to be called, is also false. It is quite impossible to develop a satisfactory theory of abstraction with only two terms. A third term, labour, as a potential unity of needs and capacities, has to be added. This overcomes the theoretical inconsistencies of the dyadic approach, anchors the theory of abstraction in social terms which change with historical development, and dispenses with all natural essences.

SOCIAL FORM

History is built upon the foundation of labour which is the only means through which men appropriate nature. It is through labour that men take possession of the world and turn natural materials into products that satisfy needs. For this reason labour is the rational kernel of society. But private property interrupts things since it is built upon a separation of men from the world around them. It interposes itself first as a wedge that forces men apart from nature, and then as a pressure that welds them together. Separation and union occur simultaneously through the establishment of subjects and objects of property. Thus private property has two sides to it corresponding to fundamental aspects of abstraction: first, separation; second, uniformity. As subjects of property all men are equivalent and move on the same plane.

In capitalist society abstraction swamps rationality. The intercourse of men with nature is interrupted, and transformed into the exchange of commodities. Subjectivity and objectivity are social forms. The process of abstraction and the constitution of these social forms are one and the same: *form is the crystallisation of abstraction*.

Consider the familiar process of weighing, where a loaf of bread, for example, is placed on one scale and some pieces of iron on the other. When the scales balance the weight of the iron equals that of the bread, but putting the quantitative aspect to one side, consider the grounds upon which it is established. The weight of the bread is first of all a natural quality of the bread: an integral part of its make-up which cannot *actually* be removed without destroying the bread. However, it can be *formally* separated from the bread and given objective existence. By weighing, the weight of the bread is given a second form of existence as pieces of iron. In one sense these pieces are not the weight of the bread; they are not its actual weight, which remains integral to the bread. But in another sense they are its weight – its *formal* weight. Four fundamental aspects of abstraction and the establishment of form are involved here.

(1) The formalisation of the quality of a thing does not create that quality in the first place, but merely gives it a distinct and separate shape. Weighing a loaf does not create its weight, but gives this weight a second form of being which is distinct and has nothing bread-like about it.

(2) The formal existence of a thing is as real as its original or natural

existence: the formal weight of a loaf is as real as its actual weight.

(3) The process of formalisation is one of abstraction in two respects: (a) the formalisation of the quality of a thing requires its separation from that thing: the formal weight of the bread is something apart from the bread itself; (b) in its formal existence a thing becomes no different from other formalised things. It is not only bread that can be weighed but many other items – sugar, tea, coal, etc. And when they are all weighed, they become the same as each other and move on the same plane as equivalents. In their formal existence as weight, bread, sugar, tea, coal, etc., are all qualitative equivalents of each other. Formalisation in this respect is abstraction as equivalence or uniformity – the disregard of particularity.

(4) Although formalisation does not create what is formalised, it gives it an altogether new potential. Through the process of formalisation a thing is reflected back into itself. When it is weighed, the weight of the bread, now formalised, stands outside the bread, which in turn confronts its own weight as something external to it, capable of determining its own (i.e. the bread's) existence. Once the weight of a loaf is formalised, it becomes possible to organise baking according to the criterion of weight.

Simple though this metaphor is, and misleading if taken too far, these generalisations are valid for private property and its intensification.

As rational activity labour is appropriation, the means through which men take possession of the world about them. In this respect it presupposes property: it is an act of property, but not private property, which is a formalisation of it. The establishment of private property is not the creation of property but a crystallisation of it out of production into a form where it exists distinct from labour. This formalisation is most fully developed as universal subjectivity, where the rights of property are totally divorced from rational activity, and all direct ties with labour are severed. This corresponds to (1) above: the next feature of private property, its reality as a form, (2) above, is straightforward. Although private property as a form does not have the same tangible existence as weight (pieces of iron), its reality is just as certain. So also is its abstract nature, (3). First it is a separation (formalisation) from rational appropriation and second, it establishes the equivalence of everything it encloses. Applying both to subjects and objects so as to obliterate natural distinctions between them, this makes possible the intensification of property.

Capitalist production, private property reflected back into itself, confirms the final point, (4). The organisation of production for profit is the abstraction of production from rational need.

Traditional political philosophy recognised that the formal analysis of private property was the only valid starting-point for the theory of the state. Tendencies in modern theory have misinterpreted it as *formalist* in two senses. *First*, it has lent support to the popular impression that formal means fixed and rigid. Law and administration, through which the formal character of modern society is established, appear, at first sight, to support this impression. It is tempting to imagine the formal structure of society as the framework of a modern office block that determines the space within which activities take place, and even the activities themselves. But while this image catches the determinate power of formalisation and its systemic character, its fluidity is missed. A more appropriate image of the formality of modern society is mathematics, which combines coherence and movement. In mathematics axioms are elaborated without being fundamentally altered. The axiom of capitalist society is the single universal form of private property: but this comprises a series of formal elements in continuous flux and development. This gives a *second* false impression, that the capacity of a form to be elaborated is the capacity of the form to elaborate itself according to a logic all its own (teleology).

Labour, and labour alone, it must be stressed, is the mainspring of history. While the formal structure of society is fluid and carries the potential for change, labour carries not only potential but the capacity to realise it. In capitalist society immediate initiative has passed entirely out of the hands of the producers: nevertheless, final responsibility for social production and its development rests in the lap of social labour. The potential of labour to set itself in motion stems from its nature as purposive activity, a dialectic of needs and capacities, which establishes both the conditions of progress and the real possibilities for achieving it. The abstraction of labour frustrates this by interrupting the direct relation of needs and capacities, and replacing it with the formalised relation of private property intensified into wage labour. But it never finally stops the movement. Nor is abstraction a single act that achieves its end once and for all. Thus the process of abstraction has to be continually renewed in ever changing conditions, and it is this that gives rise to the continuous elaboration of forms. The superficial complexity of modern society does not derive from law, administration or any other formal element; nor is it the spontaneous consequence of the division of labour and the development of social production. It arises as a response of formalisation to real development. Advances in social production tend towards a simplification of social processes as they bring closer the possibility of abundance where needs are directly related to capacities. But it is precisely this possibility that modern society must frustrate. The formal complexity of society is the sign of its potential simplification – an index of the forces pressing against it.

THE STATE

From the sixteenth to the eighteenth century political thought placed the analysis of private property and contract at the heart of the theory of the state. The most important contributors to the tradition of natural law were Hobbes and Locke in the seventeenth century and, in the eighteenth century, Rousseau whose *Social Contract* marked its culmination. The method of this tradition was to contrast political society where the state was developed, with the natural state where it was absent. Since the natural state was based upon conjecture, the results of this approach were limited. In particular its theory of the transition from the natural to the political state by means of a social contract harboured inconsistencies which it could never resolve. A social contract, like any other, can only be entered by persons possessing the appropriate capacities, that is by subjects of right. But as it came to be understood by political philosophers that these capacities were political, and that right could only be established through the state, the inconsistency of contract theory became glaring. In order to make the contract that formed the state, men had to be endowed with rights that derive from the state. By the time Rousseau attempted to perfect the logic of contract theory, there was no escape from the conclusion that the state was a necessary condition for its own creation.

At this point the theory of natural law uncovered the funda-mental fact of the political state, that it is self-constituting, but it was unable to build upon it. Political theory in the seventeenth and eighteenth centuries formed part of the wider movement of modern thought that included the development of scientific theory. In particular, Newton's work on physics and mathematics exercised profound influence over it and inspired a mechanical logic of cause and effect. But while this method allowed political theory to break with feudal thought and develop as a science, it impeded natural law as it came close to disclosing the self-constituting nature of the state. Within the framework of Newtonian logic, where cause is not only logically prior to effect but also precedes it in time, it is impossible to conceive the state as a condition of its own existence.

Further progress in state theory required a thorough recasting of its method which was the particular achievement of German idealist philosophy at the turn of the nineteenth century, especially Hegel. Hegel's own contribution to the theory of the state as such was severely restricted by his idealism, which prevented his grasping the empirical development of political society. This led him to superimpose his thought upon it in a way that proved inert and unenlightening. But his development of dialectical logic was a seminal advance. Hegel replaced the mechanical ridigities of cause and effect with a fluid logic whose categories moved into each other in a way that made it possible to see that what is a premise at one moment is a consequence at the next. Within the terms of this logic the difficulty of seeing the state as a condition for its own existence was overcome, and it became possible to understand and explore its self-constituting nature for the first time. This was the contribution made to political theory by Marx who, modifying Hegel's method to the task in hand, produced a far-reaching critique of natural law. Since this was directed against political economy, its significance for state theory is not immediately obvious and an effort of interpretation is necessary to reveal it. But the theory of abstraction with which Marx criticised and reconstructed the labour theory of value applies with equal force to the theory of natural right and the social contract.

The signal achievement of natural law was to place private property and contract at the heart of the theory of the state. In the state of nature men were believed to have immediate contact with the world about them, and to be able to take possession of anything they laid hands upon. This state was conjectural, but as a point of contrast it focused the distinctive feature of political society where appropriation is no longer direct but is mediated through subjectivity and objectivity – private property. In both states appropriation implies force, first to take and then to hold. But whereas in the state of nature this force is exercised directly by an individual in his own interests, in political society it is exercised indirectly, by others on his behalf. According to Rousseau men quit the state of nature because their individual powers grew too weak to sustain them; and in return for their natural rights received political rights upheld by the power of the community as a whole. In terms of appropriation this meant that individuals no longer exercised force to retain possessions which they now held as private property through rights guaranteed them by the state.

The distinction between this insight into political society and the conventional liberal view could not be sharper. In the liberal view political society is sustained through a reciprocity of rights. The right of one individual is simply mirrored in that of another (a world of inter-subjectivity), and this creates a commonalty of mutual interests which provides the bedrock of society. The state then expresses this commonalty through its democratic constitution and safeguards it with its sovereignty. According to natural law, reworked through the theory of abstraction, the reciprocal of claim, its equivalent form, is force. A person's claim to a thing only becomes an element of right when the force which defends it is exercised by another. In political society where particular possessions are held through a general property right, this force is universal. There is no immediate mutuality of interests, as liberal theory contends, but a universal equivalence of subjects mediated through their common relation to an absolute force. The exponent of this force is the state, which does not stand outside as a third party upholding the rules, but is the sovereign power that constitutes all participants as subjects.

According to liberal theory, private property is rooted in rational need and the state arrives *post festum*, logically if not historically, to protect its smooth operation as a system. According to the theory of abstraction, private property is abstracted from all rationality, and is rooted in force. The state is not a second-order safeguard of absolute property after it has derived itself rationally, but the universal force that is an indispensable part of it.

Although it is a general or universal force in society, the state remains a special force, since it is only one part of society. The consequences of this and the attempts to resolve them have made up the central matter of political theory. Rousseau, who refused to be contented with the constitutional banalities of liberalism, looked for a resolution in the concept of a general will which compelled all validly established states to exercise power rationally for the community as a whole. In the eighteenth century, before property had intensified into capitalist production and still appeared to have roots, however attenuated, in a system of needs, such a will was still plausible. But once industrial capitalism had seized hold of society, harsher realities came to the fore. Thus Lenin, working forward from Marx's analysis of capitalism, replaced Rousseau's general will with the concept of the class state – i.e. the state as a special force in society that is general only in the sense that it exercises power over the whole of society. Since this power (force) is the reciprocal of property claims, and since private property in its turn is the form through which labour is exploited by capital, the state of its very nature is a class or capitalist state. At this point the great tradition of political philosophy, which began with Machiavelli, reached its conclusion – and no significant advance has been made in state theory since. The purpose of this tradition was to disclose the anatomy of the state, and what provides the theme of continuity through its development is the attempt to produce a unitary theory of the state in terms of private property and contract.

In the late nineteenth century the state entered a new phase in its history as its administration was elaborated to a historically unprecedented degree. Starting in Britain in the 1870s a phase of liberal state-building was inaugurated in which the state no longer appeared a distant force but became closely locked into society. In the twentieth century, particularly in the period since the Second World War, this process has continued in a pathological way, so that the state now suffuses the life of each subject, who in addition to being a citizen is also an *administré*. At first sight traditional theory, which always took the form of a philosophical enquiry into the state, appears unable to cope with this development. Such a presumption is fundamental to the modernist project, which has treated this development on its own terms and merely reproduced its complexity without explaining it. Modernism can be rejected on aesthetic grounds; it can also be disputed philosophically, but its definitive rejection is the demonstration that the development of the state since 1870 can be fully explained in terms of the tradition and shown to be the natural history of abstraction.

ABUNDANCE

If the study of political society is not to be an odyssey through a hall of mirrors, an external point of reference for historical perspective is necessary. Until the French Revolution, political philosophers oriented their enquiries from a natural state, where men were believed to be in possession of rights by virtue of their humanity. The formal rights of political society could then be adjudicated in terms of these natural rights which provided criteria of reason for judging the validity of the political state as an exponent of the general will. In the nineteenth century, with the intensification of private property, enlightenment reason lost its charm as it became clear that there were no conditions in which the state could express the general will of society, since it was by nature a special force or class state. Under the régime of industrial capitalism, the shortcomings of natural law were exposed and its admittedly conjectural character made it inadequate for concrete historical criticism. Moreover, since the natural state was constructed out of the elements of private property, its use as a standpoint for criticism involved a fatal circularity of thought. Industrial capitalism could only be criticised in terms of private property, that is in its own terms, since it was nothing but private property, albeit intensified. Any critic who employed its categories could not see beyond the fundamental forms of the new order, and the only alternative he could offer to the miseries of intensified property was regression to the fiction of simple commodity production, where the separation of needs from capacities, that establishes labour-power as a commodity, was simply wished away. Faced with the harsh realities of intensified property, unregenerated reason wilted into romantic Utopianism to restore the unity of labour as an original fact of nature traduced by political history.

The collapse of absolute reason deriving from a conjectured state of nature did not remove the necessity for historical criticism, but stipulated new terms for it. Criticism:

(1) had to provide the basis for a real history of capitalism;
(2) to avoid circularity of thought leading to nostalgia, it could no longer be derived from simple property; and
(3) it had to offer a real alternative to the present in terms of needs and capacities as they were actually developed.

In the *Communist Manifesto* (1848), Marx and Engels developed a critique of capitalist society that met these conditions, and from that time the state of abundance superseded that of nature as the standpoint of genuine political analysis.

Abundance, or communism, is not infantile affluence – the replication of products for the immediate gratification of desiring subjects – since it dissolves formal subjects and the contingency of desire. Nor is it an empirical rationalisation of resources away from destruction and waste. Its possibility is directly structured into productive capacities, which are therefore not means to be disposed of according to external ends. In other words, abundance cannot be achieved through a plan which seeks to reconcile means to ends, since such a plan would retain the formal separation of needs and capacities. The planned rationalisation of capitalist production through formal reason is no alternative. Nor is it practical: for so long as needs are formally separated from capacities, the law of value overwhelms all efforts at rationalisation, and, as recent events, East, West and South, make clear, subverts even the possibility of infantile affluence. Abundance lies beyond the 'narrow horizon of right', where the forms of private property no longer exist and the human capacity to labour is not a commodity. The social labour necessary for the provision of subsistence retains an element of formality (planning) to allocate means to ends; but the terms on which the social product is made available are dissociated from this, and nothing stands between individuals and their conditions of life. At the same time this remnant of formality is compressed by the vast growth of productive capacities – the development of automatic production – which reduces necessary labour to a minimum. Non-necessary labour is no longer embodied in a surplus product, but becomes free activity. Free activity is need and capacity simultaneously – the immediate unity of labour.

Unlike the state of nature which is conjectured out of the elements of political society projected into an ahistorical vacuum, the state of abundance has a provenance. Neither its remoteness as a practical possibility, nor its completeness as a solution to politics, make its concept idealist. It is the possibility of political society whose development has provided its historical materials – the universal capacities and needs of labour, which at present exist negatively as weapons of mass destruction and relative surplus population (underdevelopment). The state of abundance is not deduced as a Utopian daydream from speculations on human nature: the possibility of a direct unity of needs and capacities arises exclusively from their formal separation in political society. Moreover it is not just a possibility given by the determination of labour-power as a commodity, but a necessity; it is the necessary, though not inevitable, resolution of subjective wealth and objective poverty. Hence abundance is not the basis of political society like the state of nature was once thought to be, but its own future possibility casting its shadow backwards and, at the same time, drawing history forwards.

2 The Theory of the State

ROUSSEAU AND THE SOCIAL CONTRACT

The division of society into state-and-civil-society that characterises the modern epoch, arose from the decay of the feudal orders; and in their debris political society began its history. European philosophers attempted to understand this history against an artificially constructed State of Nature. Although this method had its limitations, it showed that contract and private property lay at the heart of the new order.

The history of the state falls into three broad phases: in the nineteenth century, the administration of population (reform); followed in the twentieth century by the formalisation of class struggle. The theory of natural law belongs to the early mercantile phase which may be called the government of civil society. Seventeenth-century philosophers, including Hobbes and Locke, conceived civil society as a natural order, which having been dissolved by the emergence of a sovereign authority, was reconstructed to preserve its decisive characteristics. This order was proposed as a non-political realm, sustained by its own practical activities and institutions peculiar to it (e.g. the law of contract). Within the dualism which confronted philosophers, this reconstructed natural order (civil society) was opposed to a state whose origins were theoretically invisible; the state can only be understood in terms of the constitution of rights, whereas the approach of these philosophers made rights into natural attributes and therefore covered over the ground on which the state rests. This vision of the world survived until the storming of the Bastille in 1789. Philosophers of natural law reduced the state to an original necessity for men to reach agreement on mechanisms to preserve rights. These rights in turn were reduced to men's natural being through which they were considered as formally complete by virtue of sharing a common humanity. Man was thought to exist as a species in nature whose every member was fully endowed with the qualities of reason and compassion, for others as well as himself. These moral and intellectual qualities were what remained to an individual human being when all the specifics of geography, epoch and society were stripped away. By virtue of this species-being, men possessed an original and inalienable right to the possession of their own persons and capacities. The capacity to labour was extended in these theories to include the right to private property, defined as objects mixed with the self through work. Conversely, it followed, a man who worked for another as a wage labourer, and hence was subordinated to the will of that other, could never be fully rational or free. This incompatibility of wage labour with freedom is unresolvable, and has recurred as an intractable problem in the legal practice of formulating labour contracts.

When Hobbes declared that men combined together in a universal agreement to preserve their natural rights and give them permanent political form, he gave expression to the contractualism that provided philosophers in the seventeenth and eighteenth centuries with a model of their world. It was not necessary to claim that such a contract between multitudes of people and a sovereign power had ever taken place; rather the notion of contract was used as a concept for linking natural man, as a form complete in himself, to the citizen of emerging political society. Appropriation in this new society was effected through actual contracts daily entered into by producers and consumers, which at one and the same time provided the metaphor of contract theory, and made such a theory necessary in the first place. As late as the seventeenth century, political society had still not conquered the feudal orders whose residues remained integral to its practices, and the construction of social contracts, such as Hobbes's, bore distinct traces of a transition which was still incomplete. Thus *Leviathan* was not really a creature of political society at all, since he was not constituted by the contract that brought this society into being. *Leviathan* was a natural man, and his sovereignty over society was still conceived in naturalistic terms as an immediate right to everything in view. He was the sole natural man in the new order, because the contract into which he entered with his people obliterated their natural rights and replaced them with political right. This left him as the sole inheritor of the state of nature. The feudal limitation of this contract was its incompleteness; it only constituted one party, and did not envisage political society standing fully upon its own foundations. A century later when political society was more securely founded, Rousseau attempted a complete contract which constituted both its parties, and overcame the dependence of the political state on the past by developing a fully modernised notion of sovereignty.

By applying severe logic to the postulates of contractual politics, Rousseau showed that the inner structure of the contracts composed by his predecessors was inconsistent, implying, in the case of Hobbes, two contracts, one to create the people as a unity, and a second to place them in submission to the sovereign power. He stated the basic problem of establishing the 'principles of political right' as follows:

> 'Some form of association must be found as a result of which the whole strength of the community will be enlisted for the protection of the person and property of each constituent member, in such a way that each, when united to his fellows, renders obedience to his own will, and remains as free as he was before.'[1]

His minimal definition of the social contract necessary to bring this about was:

> 'Each of us contributes to the group his person and the powers which he wields as a person under the supreme direction of the general will and we receive into the body politic each individual as forming an indivisible part of the whole.'[2]

This conception of contract involved separate individuals willing their own powers in return for an alien power ('the whole strength of the community'). This exchange had freedom as its content. In acts of exchange, men are formally free to will the alienation of a possession in return for something other, which is different but equivalent. It is precisely at this point that natural law lapsed into tautology. It projected back into the state of nature the rights constituted in political society, as the basis upon which political society was itself constituted. That is to say, it conjectured universal subjectivity, which can only be created in political society, as a natural attribute, and then deduced the creation of political society from it. Thus Rousseau used the finished form of contract to explain its origin, and in the very act of freeing contract theory from the residues of feudalism and attempting a compact complete in itself, he inadvertently revealed the limitation of natural law and contract theory.

In Rousseau's minimal definition of the contract, each individual contributed the 'powers which he wields as a person' in return for an alien power. The necessity for the individual to trade in these powers arose because they had become too weak to sustain him in the state of nature. The resistance of nature obliged men to experiment with various devices, for smelting iron and propagating vegetables, but the social forms through which these techniques were deployed, most notably the division of labour, then oppressed each natural man as an external force promoting inequalities based on the differential accumulation of wealth and power. The powers of the individual natural man were undermined and became an insufficient guarantee of his integrity. No longer could anyone enjoy:

> . . . the advantage of having all [one's] forces constantly at [one's] disposal, of being always prepared for every event, and of carrying one's self, as it were, perpetually whole and entire about one.[3]

Rousseau shared the outlook of the eighteenth century in believing that productive forces were subject to entropy, and that the tendency to decay operated as much in political society as in the state of nature. Of society, he wrote: 'The body politic, no less than the body human, begins to die from the very moment of its birth, and carries within itself the causes of its own destruction.'[4] Since men could not engender new powers, the problem was to invent various devices by which existing ones could be focused to provide the greater force which the new circumstances required: 'just as a weight becomes heavier at the end of a long lever than a short one'. Images drawn from mechanics and geometry, especially the image of clockwork, are often used by Rousseau:

> I see nothing in any animal but an ingenious machine to which nature hath given senses to wind itself up, and to guard itself, to a certain degree, against anything that might tend to disorder or destroy it.[5]

Similarly, he spoke of governments only changing their form when their springs wore out.

But who were these individuals whose springs had wound down so that they could no longer propel their own weight through the forests of nature? The very first remark in Marx's introduction to the *Grundrisse* is devoted to this question. These men of nature were nothing other than the men of the civil society of Rousseau's time. It could be argued that Rousseau was well aware of this, since the whole point of his work was that no truly valid social pact had ever been made; only various false pacts: in this sense his writings were an explicit critique of civil society, organised around its central dilemma, that any action a man takes as a citizen (a member of the social whole) must be in opposition to his own particular or selfish interest. Conversely, if he observed the artificial conventions of his time, this citizen would of necessity act immorally and contravene the natural nobility of an uncorrupted will. Rousseau's critique of religion followed similar lines, that dogma projects the unity of humanity into another world at the expense of the political community citizens actually inhabit. Written in the age of triumphant absolutism this critique of socially determined evil, is at one and the same time, a repudiation of the *ancien régime* and a critique of the individual of liberal society, formed as a particular material interest confronting all others like it. The social contract which attempted to resolve a situation where false social conventions made men immoral egoists, by counterposing a true society which would produce new men, must surely be read as a brilliant but incomplete critique of the separation of the state from civil society. Its brilliance is self-evident; its incompletion lies in its inability to see beyond private property. Individuals in the state of nature were merely isolated from each other; in society they lived in structured opposition and engaged in the politics of solitude. Thus the common interest, while deriving from particular interests, nevertheless stood outside and in opposition to them.

Contract itself creates its parties in the form specified by its own logic, even though they appear as free and separate individuals equipped with will and desire. Hobbes was unable to grasp this point fully and one party to his contract, the sovereign, remained what he always had been, a natural man. Rousseau was conscious of Hobbes's limitations but nevertheless could not, by the very nature of things, completely overcome them. Whereas for Hobbes it is the sovereign who preceded the contract, Rousseau was absolutely clear that the state was created by contract, and did not pre-exist it in any form at all. But contract theory, precisely because it did not engage with real history, was always obliged to presuppose one element of its results as a condition for their existence. Where

Hobbes presupposed the sovereign, Rousseau presupposed the citizen, or at least a part of him. Although he saw that a new man could emerge from the contract, he still fell back on the old tradition of natural law in order to give this man contractual existence before the contract. Accordingly he reduced natural man to his self-determination: 'To will and not to will, to desire and to fear, must be the first, and almost the only operations of his soul . . .'.[6] For the reason that these qualities are not directly manifest in empirical action, Rousseau proposed the use of experiments to discover natural man, rather than anthropological accounts of social conditions in various times and places. Man had been deformed by society in much the same way that the statue of a god was inexorably transformed by the ravages of time into the image of a wild animal: mere observation would fail to reveal the rational or natural kernel of men. Rousseau endowed natural men with fixed powers as an *a priori* definition of their nature, so that they could enter into valid exchanges immediately, just as they stood; and these powers were directly exchangeable for those of all men, individually and collectively. This gave an immediate and concrete identity of the whole with the part. This equivalence of all forces meant that the 'general will' (unity or universality) which was to be created by the social contract already existed before it.

Not only does contract create its parties; it also specifies them as self-determining. This presented no difficulty for Rousseau since for him self-determination, or will, was the defining characteristic of natural man. Will was the guarantee of his purity, a defensive bulwark against the external and falsely social. In the social contract the will had to will nothing beyond its own content. But, although eighteenth-century philosophers had no qualms about attributing a fully formed will to natural man, they ran into a dilemma in that the more they whittled man down to this rational core of will, the more they were compelled to specify him elsewhere as an animal. This explains the contradictions in Rousseau's account of natural man, who appeared at one and the same time as a stupid brute stumbling through the forest, and as a noble being.

Jurisprudential theory and the legal practice of contract call for precise specification of the equivalence entailed. Rousseau was clear on this when he stated that the individual party to the social contract must gain the 'exact equivalent' of what he lost. He lost natural liberty and the unqualified right to lay hands on everything he desired; in return he gained civil liberty and the legal ownership of what he possessed. The loss was forcefully expressed by Rousseau as the 'death and destruction of . . . natural powers'. In an ordinary contract each party ceases to be the owner of his original property but retains his rights as a proprietor, which become vested in the new acquisition. It is the same here: natural man ceased to possess his specific power or force, and received in return the generalised power of the social whole. In an ordinary contract the objects exchanged are detachable from the will, whereas Rousseau's concepts of force and natural powers suggest an entity which is inseparable from the person of the contracting party. Society, at the time Rousseau wrote, had not developed commodity exchange to the point where personal attributes had become alienable objects as a matter of everyday practice (wage labour). But to the extent that this subsequent development involved a forcible separation of the individual from his powers, Rousseau's critique retains its edge.

By specifying exact equivalence as the content of his compact, Rousseau was the first to achieve a completely unified concept of sovereignty. Imbecility could not produce right; no one in his right mind would give himself for nothing; and a state founded through a transaction of defective wills could only be a state of fools. He greatly admired Machiavelli and Hobbes for the advances they had made in understanding the nature of power, and he consolidated their achievements. But in contradistinction to both, sovereignty for him had to remain in the hands of the parties to the contract; it had to remain with the people, and could not be taken from them. They could not submit to a sovereign power, since this would involve a contract without equivalence, and hence be no contract at all. Such a contract would lack legal force or guarantee, and could not, therefore, be a binding act capable of establishing authority. Thus the sovereign power created by the pact was the general will, an abstraction from all the particular wills party to the contract. Despite the non-contractual continuation of his work, this was the full body of Rousseau's general theory of the state. The second part of the *Social Contract* set the state in motion as a special force in society. Rousseau released the force of the body politic from the limitations of natural law: it was indivisible and indestructible. Theoretically he did not distinguish the state as the general force from the state as a special governmental force. Yet there was a gap between these two halves of his work, representing the point at which his logical analysis of the state met the prudential science of the legislator: the man of genius who was to produce the specific form of government, adapted to the historical moment and its physical conditions in order to mould new men for the new state. The gap was bridged by a geometrical device of continuous proportion among the sovereign, the government and the subjects. Whatever the size of the community, the sovereign bore the same proportion to the government, as the government did to the citizens of the state. Today the state's existence as a special force, which Rousseau attempted to gloss with a mathematical formalism, appears clearly in the state's nature as a class state, which cannot even pretend to manifest the general will.

For Rousseau the general will was sharply distinguished from the will of all:

> But take from the expression of these separate wills the pluses and minuses – which cancel out, the sum of the difference is left, and that is the general will . . . the identity of the interests of all is established by reason of their opposition to the interests of each.[7]

The common interest was that which is common to particular interests, while at the same time being defined through its opposition to those particular interests. Acting for this indivisible and indestructible general will was the legislator, whose laws had always to express the relationship of the whole to the whole. He had to act for all citizens and create laws that applied indiscriminately. If a law came about through a part acting on the whole of society minus that part, it could not be valid:

> . . . law combines universality of will with universality of object . . . the law is concerned with the subjects of a State taken as a whole, and with actions considered as purely abstract. It never treats a man as an individual, nor an act as special or exceptional.[8]

This was one of the reasons why Rousseau would not permit the existence of subsidiary groupings in his state (pluralism), since these would stand between the individual and the whole, and interfere with the relation of each to all. In the moment between the decay of absolutism and the age of intensified property, Rousseau's contract attempted to resolve the contradiction of a socially determined egoism and a valid social coherence, by reviving a pure rationality that was supposed to have existed in man in nature through contracting it into a new unity. The new universality and the old dilemma both speak to his attempt to formulate the nature of the emerging political state, although he resorted to various forms of the concept 'man' in order to set up his collective social mechanisms of contract. This inspired the young Hegel. But when the French Revolution sounded the warning that the general will could only be expressed through universal force, he drew back in horror, and attempted to impose an ideal unity on the emerging order of intensified property.

HEGEL AND THE PHILOSOPHY OF RIGHT

In carrying the logic of contract theory as far as it would go Rousseau exhausted the categories of natural law. His image of clockwork was particularly expressive because it envisaged motion relapsing into inertia. It was Hegel who picked up the categories and set them in motion again, and the method he adopted to do so is his great contribution to philosophy. Unfortunately, the way he achieved this is opaque and obscure, and any attempt to summarise even briefly the most important features of Hegel's thought cannot overcome this. Phrases which are crucial to his logic, such as 'the identity of identity and non-identity . . . the no in the yes and the yes in the no', are ample evidence of this. Nevertheless Hegel's thought was so important that even an unsatisfactory encounter with it cannot be omitted from the theory of the state.

Hegel took the categories of natural law, such as will, force and desire, and activated each of them in turn. For him nothing was real except what was active, and absolute rest did not exist. But because he only realigned the categories and did not overcome them, the older metaphysics of nature re-entered his system, just as an overwhelming and free-floating emotion crashes through the rationalising processes of the conscious ego.

As a young man, Hegel admired Rousseau more than any other writer, seeing his emphasis on will, as opposed to some factor external to human consciousness, such as social instinct or divine authority, as his most important contribution to philosophy. Because thought was both the form and the content of will, and therefore not limited by anything outside it, Hegel was able to blow it up into an ever-expanding self-consciousness, or mind, set to occupy the whole universe. His categories being always in motion could never completely encompass their object. For instance, Hegel had to overcome the limitations imposed by desire, which he did by de-naturalising it and inserting it into his system of fluent continuities. Rousseau had linked desire, whether of sensation or imagination, to specific wants and the enjoyment of their satisfaction. In Hegel's system desire was doubled and set at one remove from itself. A man's desire was reflected back to him as itself an object of desire, through the medium of other persons. By means of this procedure desire ceased to be simply a relation between a person and a thing and became transformed into a socially mediated process, a labile structure ebbing and flowing as each objectified desire is cancelled in its turn so as to make way for the next. Moreover, this process was necessarily formal, because the reflection of desire back into itself, so that it can take itself as its own object, meant that desire had to be formally constituted as an object which could in fact be desired. This objectification of desire entailed a doubling of its form: the desire of desire.

Thus Hegel established both fluidity and form and linked them together as he levered the categories of natural law into motion. The process of the formal objectification of desire replaced the former natural idea of a felt desire and its satisfaction. In Hegel desire could never be satisfied; just as the tasks of men were never completed; and the self never finally or fully constituted. Nothing ever came to rest: everything was in the process of becoming. And so Hegel sent his categories and forms spinning off into the infinite space he had opened up for them.

Their continuous motion was his dialectic, but he failed to find any point of entry for it in the real world. Hegel's activity was always the pure activity of the 'idea'. This was turned into objective action by Marx who took the critique of natural categories further than Hegel and completely restructured them. Hegel's dialectic was never geared into the real movement of history, since its categories, which were really the old categories of natural law, gyrated in space in order to produce a self-developing substance. As these categories moved, so the real process of history was left standing just as it appeared, in its empirical form. Nowhere was this more evident than in the *Philosophy of Right* (1821), which dealt explicitly with the state and was written towards the end of Hegel's life. In this work the total separation of thought from its object, which leaves the one empty and formal, and the other inert and empirical, is an extravagance of his method which had aimed above all at a unified flow of thought and object. The aim of Hegel's logic was to recapitulate actual development. The rich and fluid continuities by which Hegel had achieved this in the *Phenomenology of Mind* (1807) were short-circuited in the *Philosophy of Right*, and the result was a travesty; a model of state mechanisms sharing the characteristics of present-day systems analysis. The fact that Hegel presupposed his state to be not just any state but the high point of human progress genuinely lived out as a communal ethical whole, partially mitigated the aridity of this late work.

Among Hegel's achievements was the success with which he used his dialectic to overcome many of the rigidities of traditional thought. In particular he overcame the jerkiness which is found, for instance, in Newtonian mechanics, where action and reaction, cause and effect, are conceived as an infinite linear series. Hegel replaced this mechanical motion with a smooth spiral movement within which cause and effect became more intimately connected as premise and consequence, and were then continuously drawn up an expanding spiral so that a premise at one moment became a consequence at the next. If the image appropriate to the logic of Newtonian mechanics is the architectonics of an edifice firmly rooted by gravity, the one closely matching Hegel's dialectical logic is that of a free-falling vehicle. This new freedom which Hegel introduced into thought permitted him to break clear from contract theory and conceive political society without any foundations in a natural state. On the other hand, because Hegel did not just free logic but made it free-falling, he could never properly align its attitude to objects and in the end it crashed back into them.

In the last analysis Hegel's logic was not absolutely free-falling. Its coherence derived from its point of reference: Hegel's concept of the absolute knowledge of a universal subject. Marx later realised the possibilities of this logic-in-motion in his theory of history.

Hegel reorganised Newtonian logic by displacing the linear sequence of cause and effect. The series became curved, reciprocal, and circular: 'Every effect is the cause of its cause and every cause the effect of its effect.'[9] Two consequences followed: (1) there was no longer any point of entry for a final or absolute cause; (2) the effects became free and constitutive elements of existing power in their own right. In Newtonian thought, cause and effect embody the mechanical motion of inert masses. Leibniz had treated force more dynamically as the essence of matter, the power of resistance in nature. Hegel, replacing the old concept of nature with his category of activity, presented a critique of force. If objects related to each other through force, so that force was on the one hand a quality of each object and on the other their mode of relating; the internality of each object and its externality were collapsed into each other, and force disarmed as an analytical principle. For Hegel the relation of objects was not abstracted from them as cause and effect, but subsumed into an integral and labile process. The objects then became moments in that process.

Hegel established this philosophy of movement on the basis of an inspiration he received as a very young man. All movement sprang from an original rupture: a self-expanding creator, in a moment of anger, interrupted his process, and rent his product. The image of a primal agitating disquiet – Hegel's coda to the tortured movement of industrial capitalism – ran through all his philosophy, although it was muted in the rigid theory of the state produced in old age. Objects came into existence only to be negated, and were, in fact, the expressions of the pure activity of a free subject, objectified in order to be negated and so allow movement to continue. This was Hegel's principle of 'the identity of identity and non-identity'. The phrase itself expresses the difficulty of his thought and shows why it can never be presented in a simplified form accessible to the modern reader. Commentators generally admit to a choice between making the thought clear on the one hand, and being honest as to its difficulty, on the other. Theodor Adorno saw Hegel as the writer not of texts, but of 'anti-texts', compendia of history, science, pseudo-science and logic, assembled around a principle of organisation available to Hegel, but lost to the twentieth century.

Dialectics is not in itself a standpoint, but Hegel's dialectics were based upon a presupposition of the priority of *order*. This was implicit in the expressed aim of his philosophy to establish the necessity and possibility for absolute knowledge. Knowledge as the foundation of order is a classic theme of liberal thought, found, for instance, in Bentham's attempt to eliminate contingency from society, Mill's insistence on the necessity for central provision of the information necessary for a free market and, at a practical level, in Chadwick's notion that effective policing must be based on complete intelligence. Hegel's concern with knowledge and order was more general than that of the liberals. Where these presupposed the state and its order, Hegel enquired directly into them. Contract was the state in embryo because possession was, for Hegel, the expression of free activity. He therefore reconsidered the categories of private property inherited from natural law. Kant, for instance, divided property rights into three classes: (1) rights to things; (2) rights to require the doing of particular acts by persons in regard to things; and (3) rights over persons who are things. The third of these classes did not refer to slavery or serfdom, as one might expect, but stood for modern relationships such as marriage. The rigidity of the categories of person and thing led directly to the consequence that some persons were things in the bourgeois epoch. For Kant, compensation for being reduced to a thing was obtained by treating the person in relation to whom this reduction took place as reciprocally thing-like in turn. Hegel not only rejected this way of offsetting the reduction of persons to things, he rejected the conception of property which gave rise to it in the first place. In place of the person of property he substituted the subject of universal self-consciousness and erected it into an absolute, which, as self-expanding mind or substance, was to encompass the whole universe and could never become a thing to be alienated as an object. But this begged the question that Kant had at least faced up to: that in the modern epoch people were not only subjects but also objects (i.e. wage labour). Hegel could not avoid this problem, which is the Achilles' heel of the theory of right, but at the same time he could not resolve it, and in one sense his philosophy is a continual waltz round it.

Hegel attempted, but failed, to obliterate Kant's self as a transcendental category or ego, set over and against all objectivity; nor could he finally get rid of the absolute density Kant accorded to things. In order for self-consciousness to be ever expanding, it had to engage in a formal process of taking itself as an object, in fact as *the* object, the only one available to it. Hegel could not solve this problem and all he did was to transfer the density of things (the impenetrable opacity of being) across to the subjective side. The subject had priority in Hegel's system of self-expanding mind and had to be endowed with substantial being in order to free it from the empty formality of Kant's transcendental ego. Thus the anti-body of nature intruded as unexpected ballast weighing down a whole system which had been designed for free movement. This became clear each time Hegel related self-consciousness back to external conditions; in other words, each time he touched on the problem of human labour and the particularities deriving from it. Hegel showed that self-consciousness (the self taking the self as object) was grounded in the state, which established its necessary formal conditions. External conditions were things in the process of becoming objects, that is, waiting for subjects to take hold of them. These adjustments to Kant's person and thing categories were necessary in order to get them moving. However, Hegel linked his subjects and objects through the category, *activity*, a sort of pure motion capable of negating (consuming and reproducing) the objects to which it was directed. The person actively laboured to transform materials, imprinting the self upon them and absorbing them into the personality. The weakness of this conception is that this pure activity of mind, by virtue of its general nature and purity, conducted the brute existence of things (inert nature) into the core of the self and therefore into the rational totality, mind, from which Hegel had hoped to expel it. Thus the principle of self-expansion, mind, was corrupted and deadened by inert anti-body in the very attempt to give it the substance it had lacked in natural law. Hegel's motion failed in the end to move the real, and the property categories of natural law remained unscathed: the opaque thing-in-itself quality of external objects was shifted across to the subjective side of the balance sheet, where it sabotaged the viability of idealist reason with which Hegel had hoped to replace the rational harmony of persons and things. At one point in his famous discussion of the master and servant dialectic, Hegel presented this activity of combined human self-consciousness as itself an object, an 'absolute thing', which was, in fact, the state in one of its two aspects; the second being the state as individual wealth. For Hegel, state power could be expressed either as a collective product or as individual wealth.[10]

The problem of the nature of activity helped to define what later became the concept of labour-power, the objectification of historically developed capacities to labour; but Hegel himself did not do this. As an objective idealist his principle of totality was mind, and not labour. Mind constituted itself through self-expansion, and labour was pushed aside as being one means amongst others of linking mind to its objects, and thereby deprived of its status as the unity of needs and capacities. For instance, Hegel's concept of abstract labour, as labour abstracted from the direct needs of the labourer, never went beyond a description of the actual division of labour. This was fully recognised in its empirical squalor and misery, but was not founded in the concept of the capacity to labour as a state-constructed object of consumption. The process of abstraction which Hegel depicted was dissolved into the overarching rationality of the self-expansion of mind, via the state as ethical community, and was not treated as a real historical phenomenon.

Hegel also negotiated various ambiguities surrounding his treatment of services involving human faculties as if they were objects appropriate to contracts of sale and purchase. He seemed not to have realised that the objectification of these capacities as property, meant the objectification of the person in a sense quite other than his one of the establishment of objects through the pure activity of a free self.

Hegel took the categories of natural law and submitted them to a dialectic which failed to transform them. On the one side, the person was subsumed into a process of expanding self-consciousness; on the other, the thing became an object, in the sense of being the objectification of the activity of an absolutely free subject. But the opacity of natural law was not overcome. The very activity of the person polluted mind as the idealist conceives it. The movement undermined itself, like a balloon filling with gas, but at the same time taking on board chunks of concrete. Everything remained as it was. It was Marx who confronted this unresolved quantum of nature in Hegel, and put the categories of natural law into a real relation with real objects. He did this by showing that human capacities are formally objectified by the state in order to create objects in a process of production, objects whose very density embodies the value of other objects.

Ultimately Hegel explicitly cut his dialectic short in his theory of the state.[11] Right, including the right to property, was an abstraction until it was made concrete in the state, which had the impossible task of making objects of property appear as the true embodiment of free self-consciousness. And at this point Rousseau's problem re-surfaced: the state must have sovereignty over civil society, and at the same time be a valid expression of the will of that society. Hegel was too honest to fall back on the idea that this problem could be resolved through the machinery of democratic assemblies. Having developed his model of civil society based on abstract labour rooted in the system of needs, and generating categories of property (e.g. landowner, professional, artisan), he constructed the state as a sort of flow chart which linked the limited particularities of this civil society to his overarching concept of rational mind. To do this he inserted his various categories of property into the mechanism in forms whereby they would be susceptible to it. Thus the professions and producers appeared in the form of the officials of the various professional associations. They entered the state bureaucratically, so that the supposedly rational state bureaucracy could act upon them. This had the effect of perpetuating them as semi-feudal estates. They already had the characteristics of a state within civil society before they entered Hegel's state mechanism. Conversely, in as much as the mechanics of the rational state were embodied in its bureaucracy, this state had to share the characteristics of the very civil society it was supposedly transforming. The categories of property therefore only entered Hegel's state machine statically, in a way which precluded their transformation and allowed them to perpetuate the non-rational particularity of civil society within the state. Natural law property remained after all an undissolved brute reality within Hegel's thought. The state failed to culminate in the true ethical community through incorporating the natural world where, in Hegel's phrase, 'self-contained individuals associated as a community of animals'.[12]

The focus of these contradictions in Hegel's state model is the legislature, which was conceived as being part of the constitution, and thus constituted, while at the same time being constitutive or active. On the one hand, it was an element in the state mechanism, an official meeting ground for reason and society; but on the other, it appeared to have the power to restructure the whole. Because lines of connection flowed back from the legislature into civil society via the corporate representatives, it can be seen as Hegel's concession to orthodox liberal constitutionalism. Although he constructed a theory of the state that went well beyond the remarks he made about it in the *Phenomenology*, it is in many ways little more than an intellectual curiosity. It is doubtful whether it would receive the attention it does today had it not been subjected to detailed analysis by Marx, whose critique of the *Philosophy of Right* remains definitive, and represents the first statement of Marxism as a distinct body of theoretical work.

An unbroken continuity of thought links this critique with the economic writings of the late 1850s and 1860s. In the *Critique of Hegel's 'Philosophy of Right'* (1843), Marx took Hegel's duality, wherein a political state externally determines the cohesion of civil society, of which it is supposed to be the true expression, and showed that he had failed to establish them as the integral and lived unity claimed. Marx demonstrated that the abstraction of the activities of individuals in civil society was embodied in a real structure, and that this itself was part of society, and not the mediation of an ideal spirit of rationality. It was from Hegel that Marx inherited the modern state as a specific object of analysis, in the sense of a self-constituting political structure. This is clear in Marx's early polemic on the limitations inherent in post-Napoleonic measures to emancipate the Jews from legal disabilities.[13] Anyone, he argued, who saw emancipation in terms of the problem of how a Christian state should deal with minority religions (tolerance), misunderstood the nature of the modern state. A Christian state would merely be an undeveloped state, which had not yet rendered itself unitary in the face of all particular interests, and which could not do so until Christianity itself had been transformed (in social organisation at least) into a particular interest like any other. In these terms the emancipation of the Jews in the political state was limited to the conversion of Jewishness into a private interest, which was not true emancipation at all. But although Marx's theory of the state originated with the critique of Hegel, it could not be fully developed until he had gone back beyond Hegel and confronted the categories of natural law.

MARX AND THE THEORY OF ABSTRACTION

From the surviving manuscripts it appears that Marx never subjected Rousseau's *Social Contract* to the same searching critique as Hegel's *Philosophy of Right*. Given the importance of Rousseau, Marx made remarkably few references to his work, but on reflection this is less surprising than it appears at first sight. Towards the end of the 1840s Marx turned his attention from the traditional objects of political philosophy towards the new field of political economy, and these studies occupied the remainder of his life. But this turn of attention was nothing more than a change of emphasis. On the first page of the introduction to the *Grundrisse* (1858), Marx made the connection between political philosophy and political economy: 'Smith and Ricardo still stand with both feet on the shoulders of eighteenth-century prophets', he wrote with direct reference to Rousseau.[14] For Marx, nineteenth-century political economy was the continuation of the philosophy of natural law which flourished from the sixteenth to the eighteenth centuries, so that the critique of political economy, i.e. *Capital* (1867), contributed directly to the tradition of political philosophy.

Ricardo's work, *The Principles of Political Economy and Taxation* (1817), marks a watershed in the history of social thought. Its aim went well beyond the distributive mechanisms of capitalism to a theory of modern society in terms of labour as its unitary element. It contained the most complete and systematic account of the labour theory of value, and removed the inconsistencies of earlier authors, notably Adam Smith. Alongside Rousseau's *Social Contract* it stands at the culmination of the philosophy of natural law. The theoretical roots of Ricardo's theory of value in natural law are made explicit by his recourse to the 'early stages of society' in order to demonstrate his fundamental proposition that 'the exchangeable value of . . . commodities . . . depends almost exclusively on the comparative quantity of labour expended upon each'.[15] On this matter Ricardo followed Adam Smith and cited the latter's celebrated statement with approval – 'this is really the foundation of the exchangeable value of all things'.

> . . . in that early and rude state of society which precedes both the accumulation of stock and the appropriation of land, the proportion between the quantities of labour necessary for acquiring different objects seems to be the only circumstance which can afford any rule for exchanging them for one another. If, among a nation of hunters, for example, it usually costs twice the labour to kill a beaver which it does to kill a deer, one beaver should naturally exchange for, or be worth, two deer. It is natural that what is usually the produce of two days' or two hours' labour should be worth double of what is usually the produce of one day's or one hour's labour.[16]

In his efforts to disclose the general nature of the processes that govern social relations in political society, Ricardo, like Adam Smith, remained firmly within that tradition which started its enquiries through a conjectured natural history. Like his predecessors Ricardo approached the political society of intensified property (capitalism) from a natural or rude state defined precisely by the absence of such property. Just as contract theory excluded the state as the original source of right, so classical political economy set to one side the very conditions which generated its objects of study. Thus in the rude state, the starting-point of the labour theory of value, there was no rent because land had not been appropriated;

no profit because stock had not accumulated; and no wages because every man was immediately free to acquire real property. All that existed in the early stages of society were men and the world about them. Yet life in this state was far from chaotic: on the contrary, men entered into such systematic relations with each other (exchange) that it was possible to discern the law that governed them, i.e. equal quantities of labour. Ricardo took the transition from the natural to the political state as read, and by putting this problem to one side, evaded the logical difficulty of contract theory – that men must be the subject of rights before they set up the state which establishes these rights. But the problems he subsequently encountered when trying to explain profits, wages and rent are identical.[17] The logical inconsistencies of Rousseau's contract and Ricardo's theory of profit have a common origin and structure. Every attempt to explain political society from a naturalistic standpoint which ignores its concrete history, produces theory flawed by logical inconsistency. Political society is not determined by an absolute, ahistorical nature or reason.

The theory of value which Ricardo inherited from Adam Smith was that commodities exchange with each other in proportion to 'the quantities of labour necessary for acquiring them'. But if the amounts of labour contained in commodities are 'the only circumstance which can afford any rule' for determining the terms of exchange, it follows that the activity of labour also provides the basis upon which exchange occurs in the first place. The amount of labour an individual puts into a commodity not only determines its 'exchangeable value', it also establishes the property right of the individual in that commodity. Thus just below the surface of Ricardo's political economy is the naturalistic supposition that labour establishes the rights of property directly. In a state where everything is freely available men take possession of things directly with their labour, and by this physical act immediately transform them into social objects of private property. In the nineteenth century, political economy fashioned this doctrine into a modern discipline, but it originated much earlier. Marx traced it back to Locke whose view, he claimed, was 'all the more important because it was the classical expression of bourgeois society's ideas of right as against feudal society, and moreover his philosophy served as the basis for all the ideas of the whole of subsequent English political economy'.[18] In support he cited a number of remarks Locke made on this subject:

Though the *earth*, and all inferior creatures, be common to all men, yet every man has a property in his own person: this nobody has any right to but himself. The labour of his body, and the work of his hands, we may say, are properly his. Whatever he removes out of the state that nature has provided and left it in, he hath mixed his labour with, and joined it to something that is his own, and thereby makes it his own property.[19]

For Locke who shunned that extremism of thought which distinguishes philosophy from apologetics, the state of nature had its 'inconveniences', but was essentially 'congenial'. For this reason he provided a greater inspiration for political economy than Hobbes, who took the concept of natural right to its logical conclusion. Whereas for Hobbes natural right was uncontrolled and negated itself – 'every man has a right to everything; even to one another's body'; for Locke natural right controlled itself by virtue of the fact that it could only be established through labour.

The measure of property has been well set *by the extent of men's labour*, and the conveniences of life: no man's labour could subdue, or appropriate all; nor could his enjoyment consume but a small part; so that it was impossible for any man this way, to intrench upon the right of another, or to acquire to himself a property, to the prejudice of his neighbour.[20]

Subsequently, when it attempted to apply to political society a concept of value derived directly from this naturalistic theory of property, and analyse a world where the capacity to labour was itself sold as a commodity, political economy ran into insoluble difficulties. Although Ricardo came close to arguing that profit equalled unpaid labour he did not establish the point and shied away from it. In the end political economy could not reconcile exploitation with its naturalistic concept of property and the axiom derived from it: that commodities exchange in proportion to the quantities of labour they embody. For Ricardo the problem was contained in the belief, held by all economists before and since, that the worker sells *labour* to capital. The supposition that everything is paid according to the labour it embodies led Ricardo to conclude that the worker is paid the full value of his work and can therefore produce no surplus value.

Marx's approach to this problem appears deceptively simple. It is not labour the worker sells to capital, he argued, but the *capacity to labour* or *labour-power*, and the difference between the value the worker adds to the product and the value of labour-power provides the surplus value which capital appropriates as profit. If this formulation is taken in isolation as a piece of economic theory it seems ingenious but nothing more. It appears easy to reconcile with Ricardo, whose failure to arrive at it himself can be set aside as an inconsequential lapse. But this is not so, since to conceive the distinction between labour-power and labour, it is necessary to discard the naturalistic concept of property which political economy had uncritically absorbed into its foundations. According to Locke, man was born into the state of nature as a universal subject, and, by virtue of his very humanity was defined as having immediate possession of himself. Those elements of the world about him which he brought into this sphere of possession by mixing with his labour, became *ipso facto* objects of private property. In other words, the rights to specific objects of property flowed from a universal subjectivity given by nature. The mediation between this universal subjectivity and specific acts of ownership was labour, which, for Locke, and subsequently political economy, was an aspect of this subjectivity itself. Hence the capacity to labour which was an integral aspect of the 'person', in which 'every man has a property . . . [and] nobody has any right to but himself', could not be seen as an object alienable in the market. For this reason the concept of labour-power as a commodity was inconsistent with the fundamental premises of political economy, and it was through no mere oversight that Ricardo failed to build it into his theory. Marx was only able to make the decisive distinction between labour-power and labour by breaking with the traditional concept of subjectivity and making a far-reaching criticism of the basis of political economy in natural law.

In the exchange of commodities the products of different types of labour are brought into a quantitative relation which presupposes their equivalence. Classical political economy grasped this point firmly and saw, moreover, that this equivalence arose from the formative quality of labour that was common to different types of labour. But questions as to the character of this common quality of labour, and how it came to stand apart from particular types of labour as the determination of value, were dealt with by simple reference back to nature. Thus Adam Smith uncritically adopted the seventeenth-century view that men were essentially equal by virtue of their humanity, and deduced the equivalence of different labours directly from it. Employing a logic, the reverse of Marx's, he argued that the difference between one type of labour and the next arose entirely from the division of labour in political society. Thus the equivalence of different labours upon which the exchange of commodities rested, was taken as a natural datum underlying the division of labour. Being natural this equivalence did not require political constitution. But this principle of natural equivalence encountered insuperable difficulties when it was incorporated into the labour theory of value, where it had a function quite beyond its capacity. Exchange always involves definite quantities so that it is necessary, at one and the same moment, to explain the character of the common labour that forms the basis of equivalence and to determine its amounts in different commodities. But labour treated as a universal and natural attribute cannot be measured against the formal yardstick of money,[21] and political economy, having no solution to hand, simply side-stepped the problem with a pragmatic formula. Thus Adam Smith wrote:

> But it is not easy to find an accurate measure, either of hardship or ingenuity [i.e. labour]. In exchanging, indeed, the different productions of different sorts of labour for one another, some allowance is commonly made for both. It is adjusted, however, not by any accurate measure, but by the higgling and bargaining of the market, according to that sort of rough equality which, though not exact, is sufficient for carrying on the business of common life.[22]

Ricardo was equally evasive:

> The estimation in which different qualities of labour are held comes soon to be adjusted in the market with sufficient precision for all practical purposes.[23]

At the very start of its enquiries political economy was confronted with the consequences of its naturalistic premises: attempting to explain exchange (the market) in terms of labour, it was forced at the outset to go into reverse and use the market to determine the quantity of labour. This problem and the attempt at a solution recur in all the writings of natural law, where, time after time, the origins and mechanisms of political society are explained pragmatically in terms derived from the finished forms of this society.

In so far as they reverted to this procedure of explaining political society in its own terms, theories of natural law strained towards an understanding of it as self-constituting. But because they did so inadvertently rather than making the issue explicit, they lapsed into serious inconsistency. It was Hegel who moved social theory forward by grasping the self-constituting nature of political society through the medium of a dialectical logic. This stressed not the interdependence of things but the fluidity of their movement to and from each other, liberating thought from a mechanical conception of cause and effect, and making it possible to see premises as consequences and consequences as premises in a way that overcame the problems of natural law. But he could not complete the task and it was left to Marx to take the decisive step of reconstructing natural law into the theory of abstraction. The fact that he did this through a critique of political economy rather than political philosophy does not reduce the scale of his achievement; nor should it be advanced to support the specious claim that he had no theory of the state.[24]

In the *Critique of Hegel's Philosophy of Right*, Marx made clear his position that the political state and capitalist production were both rooted in the process of abstraction. 'The abstraction of the state belongs only to modern times', he wrote, 'because the abstraction of private life [i.e. social production] belongs only to modern times. The abstraction of the political state is a modern product.'[25] It took him a further quarter of a century to consolidate this position, for it was only in *Capital* that he completed the theory of abstraction which had formed the central theme of his early writings.

In his correspondence about *Capital*, in his notes and plans for the work, Marx made several allusions to method, some quite eliptical and open to various interpretations; but unfortunately he did not gather them together into a systematic work. He never wrote a theory of abstraction as such, and his general theory of capitalist society (and the state) has to be derived from the concepts established for the analysis of capitalist production. These concepts – the commodity and the twofold character of labour; value, the value-form and money; surplus value and capital; labour-power and labour – are developed in the opening chapters of *Capital*. The theory of abstraction which determines these concepts can be summarised under three headings: (1) equivalence; (2) form; and (3) intensification. Underlying each moment of the theory is the fully conscious position that Marx inherited from Hegel, that political society is self-constituting in the sense that it establishes the general conditions of its existence as part of its actual processes. If it were necessary to single out one element of the theory as decisive for dialectical materialism, it would be this interpretation of capitalist society and the logic through which it is given coherent expression. It was from here that Marx made the seminal break from political economy and natural law.

(1) *Equivalence*: by opening *Capital* with the commodity and its double character as a use-value and exchange-value, Marx began at the same point as Ricardo, and indeed, with the question that lay at the heart of political economy. But in the very first sentence he made his differences with political economy clear: where Smith and Ricardo began their analyses with the rude or natural state, Marx indicated that his object of study was capitalist society and that the individual commodity was the 'elementary form' of 'an immense collection of commodities'.

The exchange of commodities presents what appears to be a logical puzzle: its purpose arises from the differences between the commodities being exchanged; on the other hand, in exchange different commodities are made commensurable and therefore relate to each other as equivalents. The puzzle is the nature of this equivalence, where it originates and how it is established. Political economy proposed that it could be found in the labour that had produced the commodities, and on this basis developed the labour theory of value. But since this ignored differences between types of labour it required further elaboration. This was taken uncritically from the tradition of natural law and it was simply asserted that all types of labour were immanently equivalent by virtue of being human labour. Founding the concept of value in natural law in this fashion allowed political economy to set its theory in motion, but this solution to its first problem stored up insurmountable difficulties.

By insisting upon the historical character of capitalist production and rejecting any notion that its conditions derived from a state of nature, Marx was obliged to find the origins of equivalence within capitalist society itself. He achieved this through a detailed examination of the logic of exchange and demonstrated that equivalence is established by the transaction itself. Where political economy looked to an elemental labour preceding all specialisation as the principle of equivalence, Marx took this specialisation, enhanced by the division of labour, as the precipitant of the exchange that produced the conditions of equivalence. He used the simple example of a weaver who exchanges ten yards of linen for a coat. As use-values the linen and the coat are different: so are the labours that produce them – weaving and tailoring. Admittedly they are immanently equivalent in so far as the weaver could put his hand to tailoring and make a coat for himself, but this is insufficient to account for their actual equivalence in exchange. Marx reasoned this equivalence as follows: the weaver performs one type of concrete labour whose product is ten yards of linen; the tailor another which produces a coat. In exchange the weaver acquires the coat: he does this by weaving and exchanging the product of that labour, but it as though he had tailored the coat himself. In this sense weaving is the equivalent of tailoring, and the general point was established: in a situation of general exchange one type of labour becomes a means of acquiring the product of every other type of labour, so that all labours become equivalent to each other. Equivalence is the basis of exchange, but at the same time it is exchange which establishes equivalence.

The equivalence of labour established through the exchange of commodities does not reduce the particularities of concrete labour (weaving, tailoring) to uniformity: on the contrary, it is the development of these particularities through the division of labour and the specialisation of producers, that precipitates exchange. As equivalents of each other, different types of labour lose all features of particularity and count simply as labour-in-general; but this equivalence is initially established at such a distance from concrete labour that it leaves the particularities untouched. For Marx the equivalence of labour was not the whittling away of the particularities of concrete labour to an elemental labour: it was a formal abstraction. Through the exchange of commodities the general quality of labour was formally separated from the particularities of concrete labour and set alongside them as a second and abstract character. On this point Marx made his sole claim to originality in the whole of *Capital*: 'I was the first to point out and examine critically this two-fold nature of the labour in commodities.'[26]

(2) *Form*: Marx used the same example to illustrate the second stage of the theory of abstraction, pointing out simplicity as the main difficulty. At first sight, simple exchange appears to be a symmetrical relation: whether it is read as ten yards of linen for a coat, or a coat for ten yards of linen, makes no difference and seems to say all that can be said. But switching the commodities from side to side,

Marx argued, makes no difference to the structure of the exchange relation as such. Whichever way it is taken, one commodity occupies the *relative form* and the other the *equivalent form*. As a coat for ten yards of linen, the coat relates its value to the linen, while the linen acts as the equivalent. Marx drew the analogy with weight: bread placed on one scale relates its weight to pieces of iron on the other, which act as the equivalent of this weight. The pieces of iron can only do this because they have weight like the bread. But the actual equivalent of the weight of the bread is not the weight of the iron, but the iron itself. Thus it is with the value relation: the linen can only stand as the equivalent of the value of the coat, because, like the coat, it is an object of value. The value of the linen qualifies it to serve as the equivalent of the value of the coat, but the actual equivalent of this value is not the value of the linen, but the linen itself – the linen as a use-value. In the process it ceases to be simply a thing and becomes the physical incarnation of abstract labour. 'The problem is already solved', declared Marx. Through the value relation different labours are established as equivalents: through the value-form this equivalence acquires objective existence as a thing. A social capacity is formalised as an object and takes its place in the world among other objects.

In keeping with his method which made capitalist production his object of study, Marx eschewed all interest in simple commodity production, 'isolated' and 'accidental' exchange. He refused to treat the simple relation of value as an event in itself, and took it as the elementary form of the capitalist monetary system. A single barter abstracts labour, but it does so in a transitory and fleeting way that provides no basis for the routines of capitalist society. The elementary form of value is the germ of money, and Marx traced the logical development from one to the other through a series of phases – the expanded and general forms. The purpose of this analysis was to demonstrate that money is a commodity, but one so detached from other commodities that this fundamental feature of its character is repressed. It was vital for Marx to establish the connection between money and the simple form of value since this is the only way the hidden nature of money can be exposed. In the simple form of value the objectification of social capacities is difficult to perceive since it has no permanence – now it is one commodity; now, another. With the money-form the problem is reversed: now the object is so permanent as to appear completely independent and have a life of its own. The distance between money and other commodities, which represses its character as a commodity, simultaneously provides the grounds for it to exercise sovereignty over them. As the universal equivalent of value, money does not discriminate among commodities but stands equidistant from them all. Yet, having drawn away from commodities, money approaches closer to them on new terms specific to its monetary character. Arising initially from the exchange of commodities and then thrust out as the universal equivalent of value, money returns to exchange, but no longer in a passive role as mere medium. It re-enters exchange as its initiator and rationale, and by inverting the order of exchange it is transformed into capital.

(3) *Intensification*: with the development of money the exchange of commodities, $C–C'$, is amplified into simple circulation, $C–M–C'$. The elementary form remains visible because simple circulation begins and ends with commodities in their physical forms as use-values: money functions as a medium of exchange, and through the movement of the circuit it is still possible to discern rational purpose. Selling in order to buy results in an exchange of use-values which retains a direct connection with the system of needs. But these two acts (of sale, $C–M$; and purchase, $M–C$) can be reversed without changing their formal structure, giving rise to a new circuit, $M–C–M'$, in which this direct connection is severed. Since the poles of this new circuit are qualitatively the same (money), everything but quantitative gain is disqualified as moving force or rationale. Unless the money acquired, M', exceeds the amount originally advanced, M (surplus value), the circuit would be totally senseless.

For Marx, capital was not an inert object; it was neither commodities nor money, but their movement in relation to each other through the circuit $M–C–M'$. In short it was the circuit itself, and this established the purpose of its own movement. The flow of capital from money to money is formally self-contained and would, ideally, make no concessions to anything outside itself. This concept of capital is the quintessence of the theory of abstraction, and is one of the points at which it is most sharply distinguished from the philosophy of natural law which underpinned political economy.

The full significance of the contrast between the circuit of simple circulation and that of capital only becomes clear when they are referred back to the commodity which is their common and fundamental element. At first sight nothing is changed except the sequence of buying and selling. Formally speaking this is true: in reality, however, a profound realignment takes place between use-value and value, concrete and abstract labour. Marx demonstrated that money was a commodity like every other despite its special development. His analysis of the elementary form of value showed that money is the objectified form of abstract labour. Through money the equivalence of all labours embodied in commodities is represented as a thing which stands outside these labours. This becomes definitive in simple circulation when the products of all labour are related to money, and to each other through money. Behind its outer forms particular labours meet in an objectification of their equivalence. Money consolidates its distance from commodities and as an autonomous object creates new possibilities. In the simple circulation of commodities it mediates the exchange of use-values: in the circuit of capital it seizes the initiative and circulates commodities for its own purposes. With the development of the monetary system, equivalence loses all traces of its natural immanence and becomes a distant object; with the transformation of money into capital this distant object reapproaches labour as its organising force.

Since the acquisition of surplus value recognises quantity as its sole criterion, the accumulation of capital places no limits upon itself. Surplus value gained through one turnover of capital is the starting-point for a subsequent one on an expanded scale. But surplus value, as one part of value, is a product of labour, and it is against this finite limit that capital counterposes the infinity of accumulation. The industrialisation of production, whereby labour is directly subsumed into the circulation of commodities, is the historical means through which capital attempts to resolve this contradiction. The result has been to revolutionise production, though in the very nature of things capital can never achieve its ultimate purpose. Industrialisation modifies the circuit of capital to $M-C^L_{MP} \ldots P \ldots C'-M'$, which includes production itself. This intensification completes the process of abstraction and reverses the original terms of the relation between abstract and concrete labour. Abstract labour in the form of money, an abstraction from concrete labour, now determines its practical conditions and subordinates it. Labour ceases to be the external premise of the circulation of commodities and is drawn into its vortex as one of its moments. In other words, it is not only labour after it is expended (the product) which is a commodity, but labour before it is expended, before it is properly speaking labour, but only potential labour or labour-power. The purchase of labour-power at one moment in the circuit of capital, and the sale of means of subsistence to workers at another, bring the process of abstraction to its climax by establishing the separation of capacities from needs as a condition of social production.

Since this separation is as much the result of capitalist production as it is its premise, it cannot be defined in advance or derived from some natural state. It is only when circulation embraces the whole of production that men take their personal capacities as commodities. It was no technical omission on his part that led to Ricardo's failure to distinguish labour-power; he simply could not conceive it. Believing capitalism to be of natural origin he necessarily saw labour as an indissoluble unity, an integral aspect of a naturally given universal subjectivity that could not be alienated as an object. To recognise the separation of needs from capacities for what it was, would have involved shattering the unity of the very thing whose integrity formed the starting-point of his science – man as a complete being by virtue of his humanity, at one with the world. With its roots in natural law, political economy was incapable of recognising the crucial condition of capitalist production, that the subjective capacity to labour is traded like an object: by replacing natural law with the theory of abstraction Marx brought this condition to light, and in the process made a seminal advance in political thought.

The limitations of political philosophy are identical to those of political economy in so far as both presuppose a state of nature. Marx turned the theory of abstraction against the latter, but his methods and procedures apply equally to the former, especially to contract theory. The most complete version of this theory was developed by Rousseau, who attempted to liberate it from the feudal residues that clouded earlier efforts, for instance, Hobbes's *Leviathan*. But in conceptualising the sovereignty of the state as a contract, Rousseau ran into an intractable problem whose logical structure was reproduced in Ricardo's labour theory of value. Both Ricardo and Rousseau supposed that formal equivalence was given in the state of nature. From this supposition Ricardo derived the equivalence of labours which served as the basis of exchange, but subsequently ran into insuperable difficulties when he attempted to use it to explain the nature of wages, profits and rent. Rousseau derived from the equivalence of nature the right men needed to forge a social contract; but it was crucial to his theory that rights derived from the state. Each understood that social relations in political society are conducted on the basis of equivalence, but neither grasped the fact that this equivalence is established by the conduct of these social relations themselves. Hence each sought the basis of equivalence in nature rather than in abstraction.

Equivalence in political society exists in respect of both subject and object. With respect to the object it is the equivalence of commodities and the labour embodied in them; with respect to the subject it is the equivalence of the parties to contracts and their mutual recognition as bearers of identical right. Thus the criticism made of political economy by Marx, that the equivalence which provides the basis of exchange is established directly by the process of exchange itself, applies with equal force to the contract theory of the state. Since the right to make a contract is established through the state, the state itself cannot be a contract. Such a claim implies the impossible position that the state existed before it was actually established. The limitations built into the premises of classical political economy and the contract theory of the state did not hinder the original analysis of modern society in terms of labour and property right. However, the intensification of private property put too much weight upon their premises and showed that the logical inconsistencies they harboured were founded in real contradictions which natural law could only envisage as inequalities. Political economy could not conceive surplus value behind profit, nor contract theory, class power behind the general will.

In *Capital*, Marx deliberately omitted a detailed analysis of subjectivity, stating in the preface to the first edition that 'individuals are only dealt with here in so far as they are the personifications of economic categories, the bearers of particular class relations and interests'.[27] But this procedure does not pre-empt the problem of subjectivity, and it is in perfect keeping with Marx's method to argue that these 'personifications of economic relations' are not natural beings but social creatures established through the same process of abstraction as the economic relations they bear: equivalence, form and intensification.

(1) *Equivalence*: in political society wealth is continually appropriated through a series of contracts. Each individual contract in this series is made between individuals who are equivalent to each other as subjects of right. Contract and exchange are two sides of the same relation, and the equivalence of the subjects who enter it corresponds exactly to the equivalence of the objects, i.e. the

commodities, that are bought and sold. In the elementary contract apparently specific rights are transferred. Thus the right to ten yards of linen is exchanged for the right to a coat, and the right to a coat is exchanged for ten yards of linen. Transferability demonstrates the equivalence of right, since the right to one object is transformed into the right to another.

But this equivalence of right no more precedes the contract than the equivalence of labour precedes exchange. In keeping with the self-constituting nature of political society it does not originate before contract as the basis upon which contract is then constructed, but is established directly by contract itself. At the same time it is clearly an abstraction of exactly the same order as abstract labour: just as abstract labour is the general character of labour in which all particularities of concrete labour are set aside; so the right to property is an abstraction from concrete possession in so far as it supersedes the possession of particular things.

(2) *Form*: the elementary contract between subjects is no more symmetrical than the elementary form of value, where one object exchanges for another. Just as commodities can be switched from pole to pole, so a contract can be read from either side – from the weaver's side as he relates to the tailor, or from the tailor's side as he relates to the weaver. But this tampering with appearance does not change the integral structure of exchange-contract any more than changing the front for the back wheel changes the structure of a bicycle. The 'front' of exchange is the relative form of value; the 'back' the equivalent form. Whichever commodity occupies the relative form expresses its value as the commodity in the position of equivalent. Contract comprises a relative and equivalent form of right. The right of whichever individual occupies the relative position is expressed through the individual in the position of equivalent. But the structure of exchange-contract is not one of mutual reciprocity where value stands for value and right stands for right. It is the use-value of the equivalent commodity that expresses the value of the commodity relating to it. Only a commodity which is a thing of value is qualified to serve as equivalent, but it is not as a value that it actually exercises the capacity of equivalence. The expression of value is the commodity itself – its sensuous character as use-value.

A contract can only be made between subjects of right and it appears that these rights express each other immediately; but this is not so. It is only because he is a subject of right that an individual can enter a contract and occupy the position of equivalence; but once in this position it is no more his right that expresses the right of the other party than it is the value of the equivalent commodity that expresses the value of the one relating to it. It is that aspect of the subject corresponding to the use-value of the commodity which represents the right of the opposite party – his sensuous character as an actual person, what Rousseau called his powers as a person or his forces. If a person exercises his powers on his own behalf he can establish direct possession of a thing; but if he exercises his powers on behalf of another he establishes private property and right. The double-nature of right, whereby the legal claim a particular subject asserts over an object is expressed in the force of another, is decisive on two fronts. It is decisive: first, in deconstructing property by showing that although it is apparently sustained by a reciprocity of interests, it is actually rooted in force and violence; and second, in showing that force in political society is not a phenomenon *sui generis* but an aspect of property and contract. Private property is not a screen which conceals violence, and violence is not a detached support for private property. They are structured into each other in a determinate fashion.

It is evident that the powers of a person only act as the equivalent of right within a contract, and then only as the equivalent of the right of the other party. Taken in isolation the elementary form of contract resounds with naturalistic overtones, just as the elementary form of value, from which Smith and Ricardo developed the theory of political economy, led to a naturalistic conception of the equivalence of labour. But treated as the elementary form of universal contract, in the same way as Marx treated simple exchange as the elementary form of universal (i.e. monetary) circulation, these overtones quickly lapse into silence. The critical point that the simple form of contract reveals is not that the right of an individual is objectified in the powers or forces of another individual with whom contingency brings him into relation, but that it is objectified in powers and forces other than his own. If the force that gives the right to property objective expression is exercised haphazardly solely through the powers of a series of individuals – now a weaver, now a tailor – it is as poorly formulated as the expression of value as a series of use-values. The same procedure overcomes this inadequacy in both cases. Just as one commodity is singled out from all others to act as the universal equivalent (money); so one individual, or segment of society, is separated out to act as the universal force that objectifies all particular rights – the prince or the state. The fact that it is the same procedure is symbolised by the stamping of the prince's head or some other emblem of state on the coinage.

Since *Capital* extended its critique beyond the details of political economy to its foundations in natural law, it applies just as fully to political philosophy. Its first chapter can be read as Marx's riposte not only to the labour theory of value but also to the contract theory of the state. For Rousseau the state was not only formed by an original compact, but retained its contractual nature throughout in its dealings with civil society. It was a contract formed by contract which remained a contract. In terms of the theory of abstraction the state is formed through contract but as an integral element of contract itself. Rousseau elided the logic. Because the state originated in contract and in its finished form established the rights through which contracts are made, he came to the conclusion that it must have a contractual nature itself. This logic lent support to the belief that the losses incurred by men on leaving the state of nature and entering political society were matched by corresponding gains in the way of formal rights. The theory of abstraction articulates the logical process with greater precision and avoids the false conclusion that because the origins of the state and the exercise of its sovereignty are immersed in contract, it is necessarily itself a contract. An element of contract is no more a contract than an element of a chemical compound is itself that compound: oxygen is an indispensable component of water but is not itself water. Paradoxically Rousseau's conception of the state as a contract made it appear much more integral to society than the general tendency of his theory implies; whereas the theory of abstraction which roots the state firmly within contract, and hence within society, makes it appear an external object. The reason for this is that although he conceived the state as something apart from society, Rousseau brought the two together again on the basis of right seen as a self-contained structure. The theory of abstraction which asserts the unity of state and society makes them appear separate because it sees right as objectively separated into claim and force.

(3)   *Intensification*: the process of abstraction which establishes the state completes this development when the state reimposes abstraction upon society. The right to form contracts which originates in society is now superimposed upon it in the form of citizenship. At the heart of citizenship is universal subjectivity, a completely abstracted

right to property totally removed from direct possession. In *Capital*, Marx defined the object of this abstracted subjectivity as a direct capacity of the person himself, namely labour-power. Thus in the conditions which define the modern proletarian, the paradigmatic citizen of the state, the two aspects of abstraction, subjective and objective, approach each other. But not as complements. On the contrary, they repel each other as similar poles of magnets; and it takes all the power the state can command to prevent their mutual repulsion from destroying the fabric of society.

The proposal that political society is self-constituting does not mean that it created itself out of nothing. Historically capitalist society arose from the decay of the feudal orders from which it inherited the elements of its objectified forms. Thus the history of money long predates the modern epoch: the feudal monarch and the revival of Roman law provided the materials out of which modern political structures were fashioned. The self-constituting character of political society should not be read as a magic whereby it conjured itself out of the air according to a predetermined logic; only that it sets up the basis of its processes as part of these processes themselves. Nor is it suggested that it achieves this perfectly: on the contrary, the bases which these processes establish for themselves are ultimately incompatible with them. Thus a fault line traverses society defined by the opposition of subject to object. When subjectivity and objectivity are forced into each other in the determination of labour-power as a commodity, the tensions of this fault are focused and threaten total disruption.

In *Capital*, Marx defined the individual worker as a person who must be 'free in the double sense that as a free individual he can dispose of his labour-power as his own commodity, and that, on the other hand, he has no other commodity for sale, that is, he is rid of them, he is free of all the objects needed for the realisation of his labour-power'.[28] More dramatically in the *Grundrisse*, he counterposed 'labour [as] *absolute poverty as object*, . . . poverty not as shortage but the total exclusion from objective wealth . . . on the one side . . . [to] on the other side the general possibility of wealth as subject and as activity'.[29] As a result the continuity of abstraction produces, and must reproduce, the disunity of labour as subjective wealth opposed to objective poverty, as needs separated from capacities.

As political philosophy sought a standpoint outside modern society from which to comprehend its nature and possibilities, so does the theory of abstraction. But where the former starts with the state of nature and ends its history with the determination of labour-power as a commodity, the latter starts with this determination and from it constructs the state of abundance as its negation. In this state the subjective wealth of labour is no longer confronted by its objective poverty and needs are no longer separated from capacities. Abundance is not mere affluence, but labour in full possession of itself. Seen from this possibility it is impossible to mistake the political state, where the subjectivity of labour is locked into objective poverty, as an expression of Rousseau's general will; as the ethical community of Hegel's dreams; or the autonomous phantasmagoria of modernist theory.

The widely canvassed version of Marx's theory of the state derives from the preface to the *Critique of Political Economy* (1859). But the picture of the state taken from it, that it is a superstructure arising on an economic base, gives a profoundly misleading view both of the theory and of the state itself. Yet it is the one that has inspired modernist theory, which has recast the problem in terms of economics and politics and ruminated endlessly over the definitive pattern of relations between them.

Modernism is the triumph of method over substance and the dissolution of both. It is anti-theory masquerading as theory. Whether it is avowedly Marxist or anti-Marxist makes little difference since as a tendency of thought it is defined by a rejection of the theory of abstraction. Dismissing the findings of political philosophy under a series of rubrics – idealism, humanism, moralism, empiricism, historicism and reductionism – it has replaced the tradition of attempting to discover the unitary nature of modern society and the political state with a complexity that mirrors its forms. This complexity, which is only an excrescence of the real, is then projected as a criterion of science. It is the mirror of modern society which reproduces its forms in endless replications. Modernism dissociates itself from traditional knowledge and the world about it and then re-establishes a vicarious connection with them. It connects itself to previous theory by multiple analogy and to the world by reproducing its formal complexity. The touchstone of its method is the symmetry of cause and effect based on the misfounded belief that the same degree of complexity must be present on both sides. Given the undisputed elaboration of the formal structure of modern society this naivety forecloses *ex ante* on the idea of its having a unitary character, and all theory that has advanced it.

One of the precursors of modernism was Max Weber, but it would be inaccurate to class his work as modernist. Whether or not he intended a conscious riposte to Marx, he considered the same materials – the history of capitalism, the state, classes and the nature of markets – from a different philosophic position (neo-Kantianism), that led him to significantly different conclusions. In the theory of abstraction, right is conceived in terms of claim and force that are structured into each other in a determinate fashion that patterns state and society as whole. In Weber's sociology this determination is replaced by analogy based upon organisational modalities:

> Both [capital and the state] are, rather, quite similar in their fundamental nature. Viewed sociologically, a 'business-concern' is the modern state; the same holds good for a factory: and this, precisely, is what is specific to it historically. . . . the hierarchic dependence of the worker, the clerk, the technical assistant, the assistant in an academic institution *and* the civil servant and soldier has a comparable basis: namely that the tools, supplies and financial resources essential both for the business-concern and for economic survival are in the hands, in the one case, of the entrepreneur and, in the other case, of the political master.[30]

The replication of hierarchies of control across society indicates the fact of uniformity but not its nature. This, Weber proposed, was rationality, but by this he did not mean the direct unity of the needs and capacities of labour, but the consistency of capitalist calculation. As the individual capital requires consistent accounting, so 'it requires for its survival a system of justice and administration whose workings can be *rationally calculated*, at least in principle, according to fixed general laws just as the probable performance of a *machine* can be calculated'.[31] In contrast to recent tendencies of modernism which disaggregate society into a series of separate discourses, Weber recognised its uniformity, and it was this aspect of his work that appealed to his pupil Lukács. In *History and Class Consciousness* (1922), Lukács addressed himself to exactly this question in terms of the concept of totality. For this reason, and because he employed the dialectical method of abstraction (reification), his work contributed to the tradition of political thought which, with other writers of the interwar period – Adorno, Horkheimer, Benjamin, Raphael – was broadened to encompass literature, music, painting and psychoanalysis. Karl Korsch,

Marxism and Philosophy (1923), and Roman Rosdolsky, *The Making of Marx's 'Capital'* (1977), fought to defend the tradition against those prepared to dismiss its philosophy as a 'dead dog'. But despite the brilliance of their work none of these writers contributed to state theory as such.

In place of state theory, Lukács fell back on Weber and replaced the unitary order of society that derives from the dual nature of right as claim and force, with an image of correspondence or 'structural analogies'. 'The formal standardisation of justice, the state, the civil service, etc., signifies objectively and rationally a comparable reduction of all social functions to their elements, a comparable search for the rational formal laws of these carefully segregated partial systems. . . . This results in an inhuman, standardised division of labour analogous to that we have found in industry on the technological and mechanical plane.'[32] On the one hand Lukács insisted upon the totality of modern society and its formal character; on the other his deployment of the notion of analogue carries in itself the implication of non-totality, or difference and distinction between areas of society that share analogous features. It would be unjust to dub Lukács a modernist for this reason; but despite his emphasis upon totality and dialectics, the distinctiveness of separate activities and the problem of their relations that fill the pages of modernism, are present in his work. Unlike ultra-modernist thought, Lukács never denied an essential unity in capitalist society, but he failed to identify its nature and the forms through which it is established. 'It is true', he wrote in a new and self-critical preface to *History and Class Consciousness* (1971), 'that the attempt is made to explain all ideological phenomena by reference to their basis in economics but, despite this, the purview of economics is narrowed down because its basic Marxist category, labour as the mediator of the metabolic interaction between society and nature, is missing.' The result was not only to deprive the theory of a 'genuinely economic foundation' but to reduce the totality of a society to an empty husk. Lukács grasped the formal nature of capitalist society as much as any writer since Marx, but like so many others he failed to see that the abstracted rational content of this formality was labour. As a result, the state which is the concrete expression of totality in political society, remained outside the scope of his theory and could only be alluded to sociologically.

Attention is drawn to *History and Class Consciousness* because it is representative of a series of important twentieth-century works, which contributed to the tradition of political philosophy and made a self-conscious effort to extend its method, but ultimately failed in this task of fully bringing theory to bear on the development of capitalism since Marx. This series of works, which includes the imposing output of the Frankfurt School, recognised the extension of formality across the whole face of society, but in its efforts to respond to this development lost touch with the potential rationality of labour which was always the touchstone of *Capital*. As a result it failed to identify the proper nature of formality as an abstraction of labour and exposed the tradition to modernism. In the hands of the modernists this failure of the tradition was turned into a positive project of replicating complexity which, because it is an endless pursuit, has not only discredited theory, but fostered political incapacity. At the same time, the theory of abstraction as Marx left it retains all its relevance and force: that the production of wealth in the form of commodities involves a universal subjectivity or right established through force expressed as a political state. This state in the régime of intensified property develops into a class state as the wedge that separates the needs and capacities of labour, and the force that keeps them apart.

LENIN AND THE CLASS STATE

Lenin's *State and Revolution* (1917) was the last addition made to state theory before modernism submerged it in complexity and brought it to a standstill. Lenin's work possessed the same movement of Rousseau, Hegel and, above all, Marx. Its most significant contribution to the tradition of theory is contained in its considerations of the nature of power, a subject where the complexity of modernism is most dense. The nature of power traces a theme of continuity from Lenin back to Machiavelli, whose greatness as the first modern political thinker is obscured by the sneer he so often evokes from Anglo-Saxon readers.

By breaking the medieval distinction between war and peace, and theorising the state from the point of view of the author of state action (the Prince) and his subjects (the People), Machiavelli conceived the modern state *sui generis*. In this new polity, power ceased to be a personal attribute of the prince and became an historical play of forces within the people. The prince represented the modern state only emblematically; and the political constitution was not a set of rules for the manipulation of power by some dominant person or group. *The Prince* (1531) was not designed as a handbook for princes to control peoples, nor for peoples to overthrow princes. The prince was not necessarily a king, but a symbol of the sovereignty which existed not only in kingdoms but also in republics founded in equality; and for this reason Machiavelli's writings form part of the great tradition of political theory, carrying meaning for an audience he did not anticipate – the subjects of the political state and the modern proletariat.

The Prince was an enquiry into the nature of the political force which was destined to create the people. For Machiavelli the internal relations of a political unit were conceptually no different from those among political units, since both sets were formulated in terms of struggle. By establishing internal and external relations of power on a continuum, he dissolved the prevailing dichotomy of war and peace, replacing both with an overarching concept of struggle which did not respect national boundaries. This broke decisively with the feudal concept of war as conquest and a rational means to dynastic aggrandisement. By contrast, Clausewitz's *On War* (1832), despite its brilliance, represented a step backwards, for although it appeared to place war and politics on a continuum, it effected a sharp distinction between them and so reduced its contribution to political theory.

In an important section of *The Discourses* (1531), Machiavelli argued that it was positively dangerous for a prince to rely on pure force, and supported his position by demonstrating the limitations of fortresses. At first, forts appeared a good substitute for an army, but this was not the case. Fortresses were force pure and simple, and left no space for political manoeuvre. On the other hand, when an army was deployed political manoeuvre was inevitably involved, if only because the army was recruited from the people. In this connection mercenaries shared in the limitations of fortresses. For Machiavelli political strategy was decisive since it was the only means of establishing the state on a firm foundation in the people: castles and fortifications, which today are called military hardware, only induced a false sense of security. This is a lesson which most states in the underdeveloped world, and their supporters both East and West, are unable to implement. For Machiavelli, rooting the state in the people meant regularising and formalising relations of force, not winning consent. Dependence upon internal fortresses obstructed this process, because it deployed force externally to order and right and disregarded their integral connection in the state.

Over two centuries later Rousseau confronted the same problem in a more advanced state where greater importance was attached to individual freedom and will. In treating the problem of force and right, Rousseau was obliged to place heavier emphasis upon the popular basis of the state, which he theorised as a moment in the relations of a people among themselves. The people made the state but were also made by it, and political force was the sovereignty of the people. For Machiavelli the people were an element of the prince's *Fortune*, that is the object and the materials of statecraft, the successful practice of which led to *Virtue*. The state was not totally separated from its subjects, but was set at a distance from them even though, to use Machiavelli's phrase, they could reach out and touch the prince with their hands. For Rousseau the state was a much less distant authority even though it was a greater force than any that had previously existed: power ultimately lay with the people. This is the theme of continuity, force and the relationship of the state to the people, from Machiavelli to Rousseau and beyond. Machiavelli set the prince at a distance from the people, and, despite the fact that the state was rooted in the people, power was wielded externally. Rousseau brought the state back to the people and sanctioned power through the general will. Hegel never overcame this dichotomy, but his dialectic that freed thought from mechanical causation allowed Marx to take the crucial step forward and see the state as both near the people and distant from them at the same time. Lenin's contribution to theory was to develop this insight into the concept of the class state.

By the time Lenin wrote *State and Revolution*, property had intensified to such an extent that Rousseau's attempt to reconcile the special to the general force of the state had been overtaken. In the eighteenth century, despite 'absolutism', Rousseau could still daydream that power could be exercised rationally and in accordance with the general will, although it was focused through one point in society. By the turn of the twentieth century the development of capitalism had dispelled this reverie of universal peace and replaced it with chilling realities; instead of the general will, the class struggle. Lenin criticised the state on the very grounds that Rousseau had accepted it, however reluctantly. Rousseau had always mourned the losses men suffered on entering political society, but reconciled himself to the state in as much as he believed it to be a general force. Lenin refused all illusions on this matter and recognised the state for what it was – a special class force that was general only in the sense of exercising power over the whole of society. If the state, Lenin argued, was a general force in Rousseau's sense of being the general will, it would cease *ipso facto* to be a political state.

Lenin saw that the function of the state as the class state was to order the proletariat through the refinement of executive power, and drew the conclusion that were the proletariat to abolish itself in a revolution, the state would lose its historical purpose and simply wither away. Marx's major contribution to political theory was to turn it from the idealism of the state of nature and establish future abundance as the reference point for historical criticism. In following this path, Lenin looked towards communism where the 'universalisation of administration' would not be political, since its task would be the organisation of things and not the ordering of people. Although he often expressed himself in terms reminiscent of Rousseau, the substance of Lenin's *State and Revolution* derived from Marx's theory of the state as an integral and specific element of capitalist production. In this way Lenin affirmed what was always implicit in Marx's writings: that the state is the wedge dividing the needs and capacities of labour, and the indispensable condition for labour-power to be bought and sold as a commodity. It is the very formalisation of this separation of needs from capacities that establishes the possibility of their real unity in the future. What Marx saw and Lenin stressed was that the achievement of this unity would destroy the state. It would be the decisive step towards the establishment of the state as a truly general force; or, to say the same thing, its destruction as the political state.

Although Marx and Lenin grasped the historical and transient nature of the state as the politics of capitalist society, neither developed the theory of the state as fully as they might. The theory of abstraction was much more fully developed on the objective side, and Marx carried the analysis of money much further than that of the state. There are several possible explanations for this, the most obvious being the urgency of the need to criticise political economy, which shifted attention away from the traditional objects of political philosophy. But the fact that the materials of political philosophy were not reworked through the theory of abstraction suggests something more profound. It is possible that Marx believed the state did not represent a major theoretical problem since it had not yet been built into the overwhelming political force that it became in the twentieth century. Although the theory of abstraction makes it absolutely clear that the state is an integral moment of capitalist production, the development of capitalism in the nineteenth century was such that it was still plausible to take it at one remove from society, and consider it an integument that would be burst open almost incidentally as a result of working-class struggle against capital. Almost incidentally, in this context, does not mean without terrible conflict; but that this conflict would take the form of a Clausewitzian war between reciprocal forces – the Reds and the Whites. The theory of abstraction indicates the historical tendency of formalisation to encompass everything, and close the circle with itself. This is evident in its conception of capital as the circuit M–C–M', which tends towards reproduction on an ever-expanding scale. Although he identified this tendency, Marx left historical residues in his theory. The question is this: since by its very nature formality cannot encompass everything, where is the site of non-formality, that is, rationality, that stands against it? Is it outside the circle of formality, or within it, at its vortex? Does the working class have a foothold outside the state, or is it structured into the state where the materials of rationality are diffused like anti-bodies? Marx's analysis of the determination of the value of labour-power provides an important clue to his thinking on this question.

The value of labour-power is determined by the value of those commodities whose consumption is necessary for the reproduction of the working class. But the question arises as to what determines which commodities and how many of them are necessary. And here Marx made reference back to an element from a past moral economy, adducing the level of real consumption in pre-capitalist society as a determining component of the level of wages. This perspective is scarcely applicable today, when it makes more sense to replace it with the requirements of the circulation of capital. While the value of labour-power must be sufficient for biological reproduction, the amount by which wages exceed this in contemporary society cannot be determined by a right to pre-industrial consumption: on the contrary, it is formally defined by the pattern of accumulation and the mass of wage goods which capital produces.

As Marx considered the value of labour-power to be determined, at least in part, by conditions external to capitalist production, so it is reasonable to think that he considered the working class to have one foot outside the formal structures of the state. If so, it is understandable that he did not develop the theory of the state as fully as he might have done, and as fully as is necessary now, when the working class has been subsumed both in respect to the determination of wages, and politically. Equally, it did not seem necessary to Lenin to develop this aspect of state theory. At the time of the revolution the Russian state had made scarcely any progress along the road of liberal state-building and the formal subsumption of producers into a population of political subjects and social classes. It was the historic shift of non-formality from outside the citadel of the state and its diffusion within its walls, that made the extension of classical Marxist analysis along these lines necessary. What in fact happened was that the theory collapsed in the face of this shift, which broke the continuity of thought and produced modernism in its place.

The change in the situation of the working class was accomplished in Britain by a series of acts of state-building starting around 1870. Three acts in particular mark this development which gathered momentum soon after *Capital* was published: (1) the extension of the franchise to include some urban workers; (2) the legal immunities enjoyed by trades unions which gave the working class political recognition of a kind going beyond individual rights; and (3) the principle of universal social insurance, anticipated in the category, unemployment, in the 1880s, and implemented by legislation after 1911. Similar developments took place in Germany, and the political dilemmas they posed for the SPD (*Socialdemokratischen Partei Deutschlands*) laid the ground for the great political split of 1919, whose echoes are still heard in the theoretical schisms of today.[33] This is the divide between the classic tradition of political philosophy culminating in the works of Marx and Lenin on the one hand and modernism on the other. In the *Erfurt Programme* of 1881, theory and modernism coexisted uneasily: Part I presenting the general historical case for socialism in keeping with the tradition; Part II looking for practical measures for improvements in the conditions of the working class within the state. This was stimulated by the possibilities of movement and progress for the working class inside the state, and was crystallised into a Fabian synopsis by Eduard Bernstein in *Evolutionary Socialism* (1899), which can be read as the first definitive document of modernism to confront Marxism. Modernism had broader foundations than the German social democracy, whose thought was itself part of a neo-Kantian movement in Europe, which included Max Weber's sociology, Mach's empirio-pragmatism, Viennese linguistic philosophy and later Austro-Marxism. Most of Lenin's polemics were an attempt to nip this development in the bud.

The contrast between theory and modernism is so complete that one can refer to the latter as anti-theory. The former, as it advanced in the great tradition of political thought moved along two axes: the first was to understand the structure of society simply in terms of a single unitary principle; the second, to understand that this principle was subject to movement and development. From the very outset it overcame an obstacle inherent in modernism; one with which it has tormented itself and its readers ever since – the problem of integrating structure, on the one hand, with history and political progress, on the other. Modernism is anti-theory, for in contrast to theory proper, it values complexity and difficulty for their own sake. Modernism is a self-conscious radicalism which defines the tradition of theory as a convention that history has made redundant. It believes that the conditions for further advance are to be found in a negation of traditional directness and the erection of difficulty as the formal criterion of success; that is, the successful mirroring of the specifically modern conditions of social life. All this, together with the vulgarisation of simplicity, was evident in Bernstein's painful critique of what he called the economic interpretation of history. Misrepresenting Marxism as a naive theory of economic forces or motives that determine the whole social matrix, he proposed an alternative of complex interactions. With respect to the theory of the state, this has a remarkably contemporary ring: 'Historical materialism', he wrote in an attempt to prove his Marxist credentials, 'by no means denies every autonomy to political and ideologic forces'.[34]

In the modernist conception the grounds of non-formality from which the struggle for socialism is to be launched have been shifted from the rationality of labour to the extension of democracy. If the former was elusive, even in the middle of the nineteenth century, and was made to appear fantastic state-building at the end, it always had more substance as a counterpoint to formality than democracy. The complexity of modernism derives from mirroring reality and criticising social formalism according to its own criteria rather than the historical potential of abundance.

Although Bernstein made a virtue out of complexity, his work is lucid compared to that of contemporary modernists with their arcane vocabulary. The contrast between theory and modernism is most marked in the conceptualisation of power, and the distinction between class power and state power. By recognising that the state exercises force generally over society, but is itself a class force and not a general force, Lenin broke with the distinction between class power and state power which has become a fetish for contemporary modernism and an area where it has developed its obscurity to the full. Unlike feudalism, modern society transacts its relations on the basis of equivalence. For this reason power is not exercised directly within civil society, and the state as a special body is extruded from it, and operates at a distance. Although Lenin is confusing by calling the state as a special force 'the state in general', his meaning is clear: the terminology of contemporary modernism is also confusing, but so too is its meaning. By denying the concentration of political power in the state and suggesting that economies of power operate within civil society, modernism produces complex models of different sites and forms of political struggle, but only at the cost of reducing the state to a hollow husk and repudiating its real sovereignty.

In maintaining the tradition of political theory Lenin never lost sight of the unitary nature of power in modern society. By contrast, Michel Foucault, a leading exponent of contemporary modernism, produces a multi-faceted concept, and tells us that 'power is much more complicated, more dense and diffused than a set of laws or an apparatus of the state'.[35] By proposing a plurality of productive powers, Foucault at one and the same time denies the sovereignty of the state and divests labour-power of its significance as the productive force of society. In place of the class struggle, multiple powers contend in a model of conflict taken straight from Clausewitz. 'Politics', argues Foucault, characteristically inverting Clausewitz's famous dictum, 'is a continuation of war by other means', and with this statement pushes political thought back into the Middle Ages.

The loss of faith in the tradition of political theory, which was the intellectual point of departure for modernism, arose from the building of the state at the end of the nineteenth century. The analysis of this development was absent from the classic tradition and has to be made good. The elaboration of power through this process of state-building was the pre-condition of modernist thought and the problem it believed itself uniquely equipped to solve. It can now be seen that this project was based upon a profound misreading of state-building – the natural history of the modern state – for a genuine historical transformation of the state itself. At the same time modernism has issued a challenge which cannot be met simply by exegeses of classic texts. It has to be demonstrated that the process of state-building, the growth of administration and the production of procedures, are founded in the unitary order of the state which the tradition of political theory disclosed.

CONDUITE DE MIROIR

Most of Lenin's writings in the years before 1917 consist of criticisms of modern anti-theory. In *Materialism and Empirio-Criticism* (1909), he attacked the polymath academic, Ernst Mach. Although this polemic does not have the profundity of *State and Revolution*, it treated that vitally important area where natural science meets political thought. Mach deployed his notorious principle against Newton's absolute space to argue that motion is relative; that is to say, that motion is a relation between objects, and not one between object and space. But as he was an empirio-pragmatist, he replaced Newton's absolute space with human thought and concluded that 'space and time are well ordered systems of series of sensations'. Human experience, he argued, does not know absolute or symmetrical space: 'Nature is a one-sided individual whose counterpart does not exist.'[36] Although Einstein believed Mach was incapable of making any positive contribution to theoretical physics, he acknowledged the importance of his negative criticism of absolute space. But Lenin missed the point and conflated relativity with subjectivity (relativity is motion understood as a relation among objects; subjectivity is motion understood as a relation between objects and man). Mach was certainly confused, but Lenin did not clarify the issue and failed to understand that the metaphor of absolute or empty space, which had inspired political thinking for over two centuries, and provided its methods, language and even metaphysics, had been shattered.

At its very outset the theory of the state joined forces with classical mechanics and Newton's theory of space. Absolute space exists independently of all the things in it. It is the infinite undifferentiated container of separated objects, each released from an originally motionless condition by an external force according to the laws of uniform linear motion. Time also has an absolute and independent existence within this scheme of things. Newton's space was endless, homogenous and isomorphic. Its symmetry was definitive: it had equivalence in every direction – 'before, behind, between, above, below'. All its parts were interchangeable, and this conception of uniform and limitless emptiness was a complete break with the feudal image. Feudal space was derived from Aristotle's cosmos, completely filled by bodies and their places. These places, however, were 'accidents' and space, being simply their sum, had no rule-making power. Bodies, moving in celestial spheres, made a finite imperishable universe, like the feudal orders of status and estates. Newton's mathematical astronomy of separated objects gyrating in empty space, by shattering this anthropomorphism, provided the metaphor of political order.

As the feudal orders exploded into uniform social space, constructed *a priori* as a single order, in which political subjects and legal objects move at will, a science of natural economy superseded the canon law of commerce. In this new science the old ethics of fair dealing were replaced by a mechanical necessity for simple commodities to exchange in proportion to the amounts of labour their production cost. Natural equivalence in political economy (equal exchange) was the counterpart of Newton's symmetrical space, and it provided the principle through which all movements in society were made comprehensible. Natural equivalence was also the principle of political theory and Rousseau constantly used the imagery and logic of classical mechanics in his contract, which proposed a balance of human forces designed to sustain a naturally based order of social equivalence.

In consolidating Hegel's critique of mechanistic cause and effect, Marx criticised both contract theory and the economics of natural exchange. Although he used traditional scientific imagery, such as base and superstructure, he moved beyond symmetrical space and anticipated the relative or curved space of Einstein. In natural exchange equivalence was quantitative as well as qualitative, and the exchange of commodities was completely symmetrical. In analysing the form of value, Marx abandoned this symmetry and distinguished commodities according to whether they were the relative or the equivalent form of value. Thus, exchange was directionally oriented, and not reversible, as it had been when it reflected the absolute symmetry of Newtonian space. The circulation of commodities was not treated by Marx as a neutral medium (absolute space) through which capital and labour-power moved according to the traditional laws of motion.

The curving of space by the objects which occupy it, overcame a scientific difficulty, for which modernist theory has proposed a different solution. The problem is, how do separated objects relate to each other when they occupy unfilled symmetrical space? Electro-magnetic theory at the end of the nineteenth century discovered that light was propagated in waves. But because they still held to absolute space, scientists felt compelled to posit a medium of propagation through which light could travel, and made use of the ether. This usage which was ultimately entirely discredited, was nothing other than a contrivance of theory. The ether was required as a medium to fill a space between separated objects, only because these objects were considered to be separated by empty space in the first place. Social science draws its inspiration from the failings of natural science as often as from its successes, and modernism, with its notion of relatively autonomous levels, has produced a counterpart to the ether with its theory of ideology.

Although Marx rejected the method of classical science, he continued to use its metaphors, supplemented with others from evolutionary biology. Had he written *Capital* only forty years later, the theory of relativity would have been to hand to provide a more adequate language for his thought, which was in advance of the science of his day. This language can express a social world where subjects and objects are compressed into each other in a space that ceases to be symmetrical. Einstein forced physics to break with the conception of linear motion and the separation of energy (motion) from inertia (rest). Newton had gestured in this direction with his theology of a transcendant God under whose gaze alone objects were moving or at rest. Leibniz carried this further and proposed that space was nothing other than order, simply the relationship between, or ordering of, objects. But this intuition was not consolidated scientifically until the theory of relativity. Instead of forces acting at a distance across space from one object to another, force, object and space-time were united in a single concrete formulation, whose structural principle was discontinuity. The theory of abstraction and intensified property anticipated this in political thought: the subjects and objects of property were compressed into each other by the class struggle. There is no social *materia media*, such as ideology, through which objects act and react upon each other, since they are directly structured into each other. Unfortunately the language of Marxism has not taken advantage of the theory of relativity, and for the most part has remained

Newtonian, spiced with the imagery of geology (levels and fissures).

Gaston Bachelard singled out conceptions of space from classical science prior to Einstein for special criticism, and regretted their influence on philosophy and social thought. Referring to 'spatial cancer' and 'disease of thought', Bachelard coined the phrase 'the mirror-stage' to characterise that phase of scientific thought dominated by reflection: that is, in this case, by the idea that space is symmetrical, so that each part reflects, or mirrors, any other part. Reflection entered science after its successes with the phenomena of elastic collision. Optically, light particles were thought to bounce off a surface in the same way a ball bounces off a wall – thus, reflection. If Bachelard had restricted his attack to the concept of absolute space, rather than generalised it to space as such, he would have made a valid point. As it was, by mounting a total critique of space, he led his followers into the topsyturvy world of Alice, who on entering Looking-Glass House found all the familiar objects of her drawing-room imbued with a fanciful life of their own. To understand Bachelard's criticism and why it failed, it is useful to turn back to natural law.

Imagine a philosopher of natural law sitting in his study looking out on the world. He looks at it through categories which can be compared to the windows of his room. Bachelard assumed that these categories formed the panes of a single window, whereas the metaphor demands two windows facing each other on opposite walls. One window is the category 'man'; the other, 'natural things'. As property intensified in the nineteenth century, the panes clouded and became mirrors, so that the philosopher could no longer peer through them to the world beyond, and all he could see in them was a reflection of the very space in which he did his thinking. Believing there was only one window, albeit made up of various panes, modernist theory assumed there was just one mirror involved in the metaphor of reflection and symmetrical space. It saw no other escape from incarceration in the room of thought than to step into the mirror itself; 'It is necessary to search not in front of the mirror, but within it; and recognise it in its essential complexity.'[37] By insisting that there must be two mirrors, and not one alone, the philosophy of natural law grasped the essential truth of political society, that relations in this society always have a double or twofold character, neither element of which can exist without the other. Thus, an individual product cannot be a commodity by itself, and every commodity must have both a subjective and objective element. This doubling is the *specifica differentia* of political society: referred to as *form*, it is the process through which a thing is reflected back into itself. In Marx's analysis of exchange-value, the use-value or sensuous being of one commodity is the reflection of the value of another. Reflection is used in the theory, but not to produce dogmatic symmetry, as the modernists assume. Moreover, value only exists socially when reflected in this way through the actual exchange of commodities. Society is a formal universe, and not a natural world. The silvering of the windows which turned them into mirrors stands for the intensification of property. Simple property is still transparent. The philosopher of natural law could peer through his categories of subject and object, and still see beyond to a rational world. A searching look into a category of intensified property merely reveals a counter-reflection of the other. The spectator sees in one mirror, capital, a reversal of labour-power (object as subject); in the other glass, labour-power, he sees capital in reverse (subject as object). In this way the intensification of property shut out the light of reason, and created a self-contained universe in which space was closed. Only by smashing the mirrors and letting in fresh air (simplicity and coherence) is it possible to maintain the tradition of science. This cannot be done, as Bachelard recommended, by entering into the mirror and becoming engrossed with its complex replications.

'There are concepts', wrote Bachelard, 'which for the moment are still simple, but one should perhaps have the courage to foresee that they will become more complicated.'[38] This prophecy has been more than fulfilled by the prolixity of his followers, who have excelled themselves in producing endless numbers of sites, levels, instances, ideologies, discourses, deconstructions, etc. Bachelard reached into the mirror, and instead of overcoming the 'metaphysics of reflection' and symmetry, trapped the modernists between two mirrors. These two, reflecting each other in endless recession, may stand for speculative philosophy, and the dominance of the consciousness category in social thought. In contrast, any inhabitant of the room of thought with an active will would smash the mirrors to resolve his conceptual problem.

The history of painting reflects the same perception of space as the sciences and political thought. The sensuous representation of space in Italian painting of the Renaissance was achieved through constructing, with the guidance of perspective, a limitless receding and undifferentiated space, within which objects, such as the features of a landscape, were distributed. As with Newton, space was an absolute which gave the painting its order: it was logically prior to the objects depicted in it, and the picture was organised to be seen from the fixed point of view of a single spectator. Inevitably this spectator was the new isolated man of the social contract: the modern or non-feudal individual. Perspective did not in itself sustain a valid representational art, any more than anatomy could produce adequate images of humanity, because each spatial image had to be constructed through strictly painterly means. But the science of perspective did act as a resumé of visual space. In the twentieth century Einsteinian physics, and the politics of intensified property, were reflected in cubism. Here, space is closed off just below the surface, and comes forward towards the viewer in a shallow series of planes parallel to the picture plane itself. These planes tend to close up, but painterly devices are used to thrust them violently apart, creating a powerful tension; and it is this tension which has replaced the infinite recession from the viewer of pictorial space in Renaissance painting. Cubist space is a reverberation in a tense field of force, within which schematised objects interpenetrate each other and are also opened up to space. Each area of space is as carefully constructed as any object, being simply the definitive absence of object. Conversely, the object becomes merely a particular way of occupying space. Similar developments took place in music and architecture.

Modernist theory has gone beyond denying this unity of social, visual and physical space, and, by reducing the outlook to one mirror rather than two, and then proposing entering that mirror rather than smashing it, has represented a totally de-spatialised world in which only one-dimensional men can live.

3 The Law of Labour

ORDER, POPULATION AND STATISTICS

In devising laws, establishing administrative practices and developing the continuum between them typified by administrative law, the state makes concrete the process of abstraction which determines its history and guides its actions. Although it is not self-conscious and makes no explicit reference back to abstraction as such, the state produces its activities from a set of categories in which abstraction is firmly and unmistakably embodied. The two most important, order and population, are not arbitrary but have their own histories and stand in a definite relation to each other.

Set in its historical context the appropriate contrast to modern order is not chaos as liberal theory suggests, but either the potential state of abundance or the feudal orders from which the state emerged. The remnants of these orders were recast under the pressure of private property to make up the modern order. Feudalism was an ensemble of orders, estates and corporations constituted as collectivities. Seigneurs enjoyed the capacity to use manorial courts to produce rent for themselves by virtue of their status. Although the feudal orders made up a pyramid with the Holy Roman Emperor and the Pope at the apex, the structure was not a continuous hierarchy; and the monarch did not link himself through ramified channels to inferior layers, subject to direction from above. Consequently, ordinary inhabitants were not citizens having some kind of direct relationship with the apex.

The most appropriate image of feudal society is of a nest of boxes each inside the other but not connected through any overarching framework. By contrast modern society is organised through such an overarching framework, like a sphere, on the surface of which each point is separate from its neighbours and can only relate to them through an equidistant centre. In contrast to the constellation of feudal orders, modern society is a single order. But the nature of this single overriding order has been interpreted in diverse ways. The historical contrast with the feudal orders is clear and revealing: sovereignty in the feudal period was parcellised, and acts of force were not centrally orchestrated, nor rooted in a general system of right. Relations were not mediated through a central authority but were made directly at all points. The feudal practice of corvée, for example, involved an immediately political relationship between producers and non-producers, whereby a serf was compelled to work a fixed number of days annually on his lord's personal estate. The reproduction of serf labour was guaranteed by his direct control of other plots of land, and he received no immediate return for his work on the lord's demesne, which accrued to the latter as rent. In the corvée, force was directly applied to the serf as producer and compelled him to produce rent for the lord. This force was particular, being applied to each serf separately, and the compulsion to work was not general as it is in modern society, where it operates through an impersonal labour market. The tie between lord and serf was personal and visible.

On the other hand, despite its immediacy, the servile relation of serf and master was not self-sufficient and could only exist as one of a whole series of such relationships. However, the connections between the relationship of any particular lord and serf, and the general conditions in which it operated, were quite different from the connection between an individual worker and his employer, and the general conditions within which this operates. In the feudal period the orders were constituted and reproduced discretely at the manorial level, and, in so far as there was a feudal system, it was simply a constellation of already constituted elements. The whole did not have priority over the parts, and expressions of the whole tended towards intangibility. For instance, kingship was liturgical (i.e. an embodiment of honour expressed through ceremony, ritual and oathing) and not a matter of sovereignty. Thus, although the feudal orders reached towards unity, they were not produced from a totality. The conditions of modern society differ dramatically. First, the unity of the system (order) has absolute priority and sovereignty is unmistakably tangible. Second, the relationship of producer to non-producer (wage labour to capital) is not personal; nor, more importantly, is it immediately political.

This is the decisive point of difference between the fedual orders and political order. In the manor relations of production were grounded in status, which brought serf and master together as inferior and superior: on this account feudal relations of production were immediately relations of power. In the capitalist factory, workers and capital are equivalents brought together by a contract whose very nature and existence expels all immediate political content. While the real result of this contract is the worker's submission to capital, it must be stressed that this submission takes place under the sign of freedom and equivalence. One crucial presupposition of modern contract, which it then reproduces, is that both parties are deprived of the right to act violently in defence of their own interests, or even to pardon those who harm them. In a society of equivalents relating to each other through contract, politics is abstracted out of the relations of production, and order becomes the task of a specialised body – the state.

The state as the locus of order, and the replacement of status by equivalence, are part and parcel of the same thing, since individuals only confront each other as equivalents through the medium of the state which is equidistant from them all. Equivalence in political society does not have natural roots in some assumed innate equality of all men, but political roots in the state and citizenship. Individuals do not take each other as immediate equivalents by recognising in others the same natural traits of humanity which they possess themselves: but as political equivalents, as citizens – i.e. formal equivalents. Social relations in capitalist society are not only not immediately political, they are not even immediate at all; on the contrary they are mediated and formal. In the feudal period social relations as a whole comprised a mass of particular relations; in capitalist society individual relations are not immediate, nor even particular, in so far as each is an exact replica of every other (equivalence). The individual relation is no longer the ground of totality but a reflex of it, an individuated element of it: its structure presupposes a single, overarching and unified order, for only this can produce equivalence. But since this order is established apart from all particular relations, and must therefore shed all traces of particularity, it is clearly abstract and formal itself. Whereas the feudal orders appear highly structured and individual relations appeared to dovetail neatly into each other, capitalist society at first sight presents itself as absolute disorder – a mass of identical elements in continuous flux. Where the feudal orders present the image of a fixed and stable structure, capitalism appears a chaos of disordered movement. This apparent disorder does not im-mediately disclose the fact that it is formally ordered. A belief in immanent disorder has conditioned the most diverse schools of thought, and turned the search for order into the quest for a *deus ex machina*, from Hobbes's *Leviathan*, through Adam Smith's *invisible hand*, to Gramsci's *hegemony*. Today modernism has reduced this to an obsession with ideologies of social control legitimacy.

The confusion of formal order with immanent disorder derives from a misapprehension of the nature of formality in modern society. Form is mistaken for formalism, and believed empty and hollow. Since the order which formality has established (the formal order) is not visible, something has to be constructed to take its place. Or to put it another way, since forms appear empty or schematic, and incapable of constituting order, a content has to be fabricated and inserted so as to hold disorder at bay and give society coherence.

Three solutions that have been proposed are as follows:

(1) *Natural property*: this is really a magical solution where chaotic movement is seen as the superficial face of a deep structure of order arising from individuals' natural rights to ownership and the terms of mutuality and reciprocity apparently inscribed within them. The problem here is that the state disappears and plays as much part in the activities of society as a linesman at a soccer game.

(2) *Labour discipline*: really a derivative of the above. Here society is seen as a single productive enterprise revolving around the division of labour, which is taken at face value as an organising principle of activities. Within the division of labour individuals are seen as directly dependent upon each other for the production of their conditions of life, and from this dependence order is believed to arise. Here a co-ordinating rationality is ascribed to political society which it does not possess.

(3) *The autonomy of the state*: sovereignty, which sets the state at a distance from society, gives rise to the illusion that it is an autonomous locus of order possessing specialised instruments to achieve this end. One of these is violence; the other, consent through ideology. The problem here is the opposite to that in (1), being the autonomy of the state from which these instruments of order are derived, since it ignores the real history and nature of the state in terms of the development of private property.

The apparently chaotic and disorderly movement of political society, which appears as a series of accidental and uncontrollable collisions between individuals, presupposes the conditions which constitute its order. For this chaotic movement can only occur among individuals who are already formally established as equivalents, and thus formal equivalence, objectified in the state, is nothing but the *locus classicus* of order itself. This does not mean that formal order is self-sustaining or complete, and one should not confuse its appearance as disorder with the real contradictions arising from it. It is only on the basis of grasping the formal nature of order, and disregarding the illusion of immanent chaos, that the real origins of the tensions of political society can be correctly construed. Moreover, the activities of the state in maintaining order are not directed against some primal chaos, but against discontinuities within the political orders. Since the state is itself constructed as part of this order, measures it takes for its own preservation, and the specialised instruments it employs, already presuppose modern order, and are structured in terms of it. Once the apparently structured orders of feudalism decomposed and were replaced by the order of equivalence, the contours of society were flattened and it appeared as a natural, uniform mass. This gave rise to the first and most fundamental category of modern political thought, *population*, a category, which more than any other, presents itself as natural.

In modern society where all the means and conditions of life take the form of a mass of commodities, identical as social objects, members of society become partners of these objects in a corresponding mass of uniform subjects. The science of demography begins here and takes this mass as its object of study – the population as a self-evident and ready-made natural entity, waiting to be quantitatively analysed. Thus Malthus, in his celebrated attempt to discover the 'principles of population', began by addressing himself exclusively to questions of magnitude. For him, as for so many before and since, the problem appeared to be: what is it that determines the size of human societies, and what are the consequences of changes in this size? He took the established idea that population grows geometrically while means of subsistence increase arithmetically, and derived from it various consequences for the life of the poor at the end of the eighteenth century. In coming to the conclusion that it was necessary for the poor to exercise moral restraint over sexual passion (to curb their natural appetites), he arrived at the issue of discipline and order which lay at the heart of the population category. Only he saw it as a result of population and not as a presupposition. The population category already presupposes political order, since it can only exist where society comprises a mass of equivalent individuals. But by naturalising population, and seeing it simply as an aggregation of human beings, demography has obliterated this point. As Malthus's *An Essay on the Principle of Population* (1798) shows, and modern studies confirm, the question of order cannot be removed from population, even if it only reasserts itself as a secondary concern about population control.

Any attempt to analyse the magnitude of population and the conditions and consequences of changes in it, implies a prior question which demography has consistently ignored: how did the category, population, come into being in the first place? This resolves itself into the question: why do the traders in labour-power take the social form of population? Population is an historically specific category, and is only appropriate for a society where each individual stands alone, as the equivalent of others. Feudal orders were not constituted as a population, and the Domesday Book, for instance, did not enumerate people, but listed fiscal units to which more or less people of varying status were attached. The category simply did not apply where real qualitative differences existed as between master and slave in classical antiquity, or seigneur and serf in medieval Europe. A population does not consist of natural beings, but of subjects capable of relating to objects. It is not the ready-made thing assumed by demography but a specific category linked to others, such as money, order, law, administration and police. Taken as a self-evident category, population is an empty formalism. As a real historical category it came into being with the collapse of the feudal orders, and was made up first of all of individuals cast out into households from the communal activities which had previously linked them to others. In other words, population arose with the development of absolute property, and, on this account is linked to the development of the state itself. As the category of population is explored in depth it becomes clear that it is the first category of political order.

Malthus and earlier political arithmeticians overlooked this and consequently failed to ask two pertinent questions: (1) Under what conditions did society come to be ordered specifically as a population? (2) Why did the material aspect of the subjective existence of individuals born into these conditions assume a law-like nature (e.g. the laws of population)? Their failure to pose these questions inevitably reduced their analysis of subsistence to an arithmetic plane which is perfectly consistent with the naturalistic basis of the companion science of political economy, to which Malthus himself was a significant contributor. At the time he was writing, barriers to the replication of individuals in a population explosion were being broken down, and the gap between the high death rate and the even higher birth rate temporarily widened. The system for the mass production of human beings was in the process of being established.

The concept of population was always closely tied to political economy, the connection having already been made in the seventeenth century by Sir William Petty, the 'father of the labour theory of value'. Once labour was taken as the source of value, population became a symptom of wealth, a cause of wealth, and indeed wealth itself. 'People', wrote W. Petyt, a contemporary of Petty, 'are . . . the chiefest, most fundamental, and precious commodity.'[1] At the same time it was also recognised that the character of people as wealth depended directly upon their poverty. ' . . . in a Free Nation where Slaves are not allow'd of', wrote Bernard Mandeville in the next century, 'the surest wealth consists in a multitude of Laborious Poor; for besides that they are the never failing Nursery of Fleets and Armies, without them there could be no enjoyment, and no Product of any Country could be valuable.'[2]

As demography was linked to political economy, so its analysis of population formed part of a more general project of quantitative analysis, which developed into the modern discipline of statistics. The immediate occasion of this new discipline was the trade in commodities which stimulated the development of book-keeping as the guarantee of precision in the expression of value. Value, as an abstraction, had to be expressed in the abstract, as figures in a ledger, alongside the actual events, such as the buying and selling of goods, which realised it. Specialised book-keeping and accounting became a necessary adjunct of burgeoning commodity production from the sixteenth century onwards. Development in the seventeenth century gave a further impulse to measurement and statistics, when every picture was transformed into a mathematical image. The emergence of population as a universal and distributional category stimulated statistics, not just as a process of collecting information, but also as a procedure for analysing probability. This new science of probability was inextricably bound up with the search for a principle of certainty (order) to resolve the problem of scepticism which had dominated philosophy for centuries. Descartes had attempted to establish a fixed point of certainty in the very ability of the individual to reflect on his doubts (*cogito ergo sum*). But from the point of view of probability theory he erred, as certainty attaches to the population as a whole, and not to individual members of it. At the same time, although probability theory acknowledged that the behaviour of individuals was uncertain, it nevertheless could not treat them as entirely random since it assumed them to be members of a population, and therefore to share properties in common. From the moment population emerged as an historical reality, and as a distributional category forming part of that reality, certainty could no longer be founded in the individual subject, whose view is always *merely* subjective. And it was another philosopher of the period, Blaise Pascal, who shifted the search for order back to its real historical site, the population.

Pascal freed chance from superstition by showing that the probability of a random event has a well-determined value, which does not depend on opinion, and so is neither merely subjective nor transcendentally determined by fate. It is thought that he worked out this new mathematics of probability when examining the gambling losses of the Chevalier de Méré in 1654. At the gaming table order emerges from the morass of random events according to well-defined laws of probability. The whole universe of events (the population) is the locus of order and therefore of knowledge, not each individual event on its own. This idea was deeply embedded in Pascal's non-mathematical work, which ironically is often seen as a sort of last-ditch defence of feudalism. 'Let us say', he wrote, '"God is, or He is not." A game is playing . . . in which heads or tails may turn up. What will you wager?'[3] He argued that since there were a finite number of chances of loss, and an infinity of infinitely happy life to win, out of the infinity of chances there must be one for every one. Every man had to wager one way or the other on the existence of God, and stake his reason, will, knowledge and happiness. Thus the gambler staked a finite certainty against a finite uncertainty without acting unreasonably. The uncertainty of the gain was proportioned to the certainty of the stake. The search for mathematical precision in the estimation of probability, although taking its inspiration from a religious dilemma, led to many secular results.

The life insurance offices used this method to construct mortality tables, and thus mobilised probability as an instrument for analysing population. The death rate for various groups was estimated and annuity prices set accordingly. These annuities were a widespread object of gambling in the eighteenth century. Another contemporary of Sir William Petty, John Graunt, constructed mortality tables to show that 36 per cent of the children of the London Parishes died before the age of six, and that the average expectancy of life for Londoners was seventeen and a half. What was a subjective uncertainty for the individual, was an ascertainable value for the population as a whole. However, the struggle to establish simple magnitudes was protracted, and the word 'statistics' itself originated in the term 'statist', meaning 'one having knowledge of state affairs'. The original emphasis was on the facts themselves, rather than on the statistical operations producing the tables of combinations known as facts.

Petty wrote of his method of study: 'The Method I take to do this is not very usual; for instead of using only comparative and superlative words, and intellectual Arguments, I have taken the course . . . to express myself in Terms of *Number, Weight, or Measures*; to use only Arguments of Sense, and to consider only such Causes, as have visible Foundations in Nature.'[4] But it was Gregory King, at the very end of the seventeenth century, who attempted to establish actual magnitudes of population in a systematic way. Petty himself tended chauvinistically to assert large magnitudes in relation to Britain's population and wealth. The theoretical point is that the full development of population as an historical and distributional category required the counting of individuals as such. This was not achieved in England until 1801 and was the result of theoretical and administrative labour lasting centuries. King's estimate of the population of England in 1695 at five and a half million was an important episode revealing the potential of the population category, yet stopping short of its fulfilment.

In 1694 an Act was passed for levying taxes on burials, births and marriages, and annual dues on bachelors and childless widowers. Its implementation required means for collecting information on an unprecedented scale. David Glass suggested that the Act was covertly aimed at a national census.[5] But the full mechanism of censuses and civil registration did not come until much later. The 1694 Act was not watertight and it was still possible to be legally born and buried without being listed. Not only was the Act defective, but King lacked access to some of the information it produced, and even failed to make use of that information which was available. This suggests that the category of population had not been fully theorised at that time, as indeed it had not been developed politically through the franchise and similar institutions.

The fact that King's career was in the Colleges of Heralds suggests how little the concept of population had been freed from feudal status. King never explained his techniques of calculation, but it is obvious that he achieved his results by a series of successive approximations based on intelligent guesswork, supported by intensive research in a few localities. Having calculated the number of households as best he could, King then multiplied this by a population factor. His efforts anticipated the future census, but at the end of the seventeenth century he was unable to achieve the literal numbering of people, because his explicit object was still essentially feudal in character – the calculation of revenue-producing capacity. This attempt at systematising feudal orders was a decisive step towards modern order. Exactly the same systematisation was carried out through the foundation of the Bank of England nine years earlier. Feudal fiscality synthesised money and population in its taxation units but the modifications of this for the order of private property required a separation corresponding to the division of subject from object. On one side fell population and the office of the Registrar General; on the other side, the modern monetary system and the central bank.

The actual principle of population, or the real conditions and consequences of its magnitude, originated in the process of primitive accumulation. In this phase wealth was turned into value and piled up as money on the one side; and serfs were turned into people and piled up as population on the other. The one became capital; the other, labour; although this clear distinction did not emerge until much later. Consequently the connection between them was not clear, and they appeared as totally separate things and persons. Value appeared as precious metal, credit and goods; labour as rogues and vagabonds. This *canaille* was thought to be a threat to property, rather than the source of accumulation, and savage penalties were invoked to deal with it. At the end of the sixteenth century a change took place and the rogues and vagabonds were no longer seen as something outside property, but as a source of labour. A century later this new perspective came to be systematically applied as the state began to develop labour-power through its administrative machinery. Penal confinement was doubly logical in this period, as it both made labour available to experiments in productive methods geared to profit; and at the same time delimited an external sphere of freedom within which subject could meet subject in contract without any predetermination. When intramural production was finally established as the concern of private capital, the first part of this rationale disappeared, leaving discipline and penality, as the sole remaining rationale of incarceration.

Once capitalism was consolidated, the mass production of human beings began to generate a surplus. The changing proportion of variable to constant capital means that more labour-power is produced than can be absorbed into the labour process. The law of population is then expressed in the pressure of producers against the means of employment. This fundamental law of accumulation, the production of relative surplus population, acts as a key mechanism of order in compelling competition in the labour market, and replaces the direct force of the *corvée* and penal confinement.

The emergence of the proletariat as a distinct class by the nineteenth century not only cleared the way for the founding of the census but gave immediate encouragement for new developments in statistics as statistical societies, comprising members of the local bourgeoisie, sprang up in many large towns. These societies collected information about local workers and inhabitants of the slums. They aggregated data under broad moral categories relating to the dangers of factory work to motherhood, the cultural susceptibility of workers to radical literature, and so on. Theoretical considerations were left to political economy, as the members of the societies were pragmatic in outlook and committed to reform.

Population as a fully developed category not only presupposes a universe of equivalent individuals but also a universal object to which they are related, namely the state. For this reason it leads to the abolition of all social specificity and establishes uniformity as the fundamental principle of administrative classification. In this way it became the central category of state knowledge: the category through which the state knows itself and indicates its own activities. At the same time, however, because it is not the natural category it is believed to be, it obscures as much as it reveals, and casts its own presuppositions, and thus those of social production generally, into obscurity. Population is the corollary of capital, but this essential character is lost once it is treated as a natural entity. As an ontological category population in the nineteenth century revealed its pedigree as natural law, modified in ways appropriate to conditions of capitalist production. The concrete expression of population as a uniform category of administration is the classification of its members as employed or unemployed, which was implemented about the turn of this century. Prior to this, and following the period of the classic *Blue Book* surveys, concepts of social pathology stimulated the development of statistical techniques within the Eugenics Movement. Among the important achievements of this movement were refinements of the analysis of means and variance, such as regression and correlation. In a way these techniques of modern statistical analysis synthesised Descartes's focus on the individual with Pascal's universe of events, into the distributional nature of the population category. From this development a new psychology emerged as a science of individual differences working through the measurement of human attributes in scalar terms, that is in statistical terms of distributional ranking. Prior attempts had been made to measure human faculties by means of experimentally subjecting the individual to sensory stimuli and recording his 'experience' of them. The theoretical context of these experiments was the determination of the link between mind and body as it existed within one individual. But around 1890 a decisive shift occurred, whereby intelligence was specified as a unitary category (not various faculties). This was behaviourally measured as a single numerical magnitude by means of a test, on a distributional or scalar (i.e. population) basis, which located individuals on a continuum.[6] It lost its absolute nature as a single instance of the relation between two universals (mind and body) and became a reflex of the population category. The shift was achieved by means of the invention of a simple device, the intelligence test, which compared behaviour across a range of individuals in order to establish interior differences. Significantly, this procedure was evolved at the very time when the population category was implemented through the classification of its members on the employment–unemployment axis. In fact the immediate occasion of the new test was the establishment of the feeble-minded as an administrative category, whose members were hard to detect. The condition was invisible, and became manifest in problems of classroom organisation following the introduction of compulsory education from the 1870s onwards. The point that must be stressed is that the intelligence test is a practice which derives directly from the statistical manipulation of the population category, and lends support to the illusion that it is a natural category (that is, people are thought to naturally have or naturally acquire 'intelligence'). Population thus refers to the way in which variations in concrete labour, that are created by capital, are made to appear as a series of natural capacities. It completes its objective of naturalising the conditions of capitalist production by transforming the consequences of the division of labour into distributional norms of intelligence which reconstitute pathology as deviation from the mean.

From the population category a whole series of classifications have been developed in terms of the capacity to labour, defined naturalistically around age, gender, intelligence and health. Although it can produce pictures of misery, due to the unequal distribution of income, it can give no clue as to the causes of this misery, since the illusory naturalism of the population category obscures the formal character of the conditions which produce this inequality.

THE RULE OF LAW AND THE EXTENSION OF ADMINISTRATION

Political philosophy as it was developed by the theorists of natural law, and subsequently by Hegel and Marx, placed its emphasis upon the formal conditions which gave rise to the state, but paid less attention to its constitutive power over society. In the case of Rousseau and Hegel this aspect of the state was inevitably obscured because each, in his own way, had to assume that the origin of the state and the full elaboration of civil society were immediately connected events. Marx, who understood that this was not the case, never systematically elaborated his position on this question. Although political authority assumed the form of the state as social relations were founded on the basis of private property, the intensification of private property and the subsequent development of capitalism could only take place through social classes established by the state through the medium of law and administration. In this respect the state is as much the premise of capitalist society as its result. The state can only act in ways consonant with its abstract character. Law and administration, which fully embody the population category, are practical applications of this.

The political life of modern society presents itself as an endless series of administrative acts. The citizen is not only a subject of rights, but also an object of administration (an *administré*). As a member of political society the individual is already schematised: an equivalent to all other individuals who move on the same plane, he is never anything but an individuated element of a total system.

Now the fact that he is also an object of administration is visible at a glance in the gigantic structure that envelopes him. This re-definition of the individual into an *administré* is commonly under-stood as part of the process of transition from *laissez-faire* to state intervention, which are generally taken as quite distinct from each other. However the distinction is illusory. There never was a phase of *laissez-faire*, and the development of administration is nothing but the evolution of the state. In this light the transformation of the individual into an *administré* is not the negation of citizenship, but the completion of its development. Any effort to develop criteria of freedom from the juridical democracy of a supposed *laissez-faire* period, and criticise contemporary conditions from this standpoint, is founded on false premises about the nature of the state, law and administration.

The growth of administration has been most marked in the so-called economic sphere of government. In Britain between the wars, there was a fourfold increase in the number of civil servants dealing with the management of sterling, trade protection, the guarantee of agricultural markets, and similar tasks. Earlier the ramshackle and monstrous Ministry of Munitions had anticipated the all-encompassing regulation of labour, pricing and capital investment. But it did not foreshadow the means by which such regulation was achieved later in the century, and was hurriedly dismantled at the end of the First World War. By contrast, the methods used in the Second World War were kept intact.[7]

Contemporary administration of economic and social life con-trasts with earlier forms of control through the law, along the same lines that a system of regulated prices differs from a free-market mechanism. Private law regulates the relations spontaneously entered into by individuals, so that in the law of contract the state appears as a third party to enforce liabilities. In public law it is always immediately present as Other. But unfortunately this simple contrast is insufficient for understanding the complexities of modern administration. Law is not a set of coercive rules, but a tangible expression of a social form with a predetermined historical content, namely the commodity nature of the products of labour under a régime of absolute property.

In capitalist society the capacity to labour as well as its products has become a commodity, and this presented serious difficulties for the law of contract. The law of private property as it had developed by the end of the eighteenth century was in fact quite incapable of dealing with intensified property in the nineteenth century, when profound modifications proved necessary on both sides of the wage relation. A new legal subjectivity, the joint stock company with limited liability, was established for capital; equally important innovations were made for labour.

Ideally the law is a form of rule which protects the citizen from arbitrary violence against his property and person, while subjecting the officers of the state to the same conditions as all other citizens. However, laws have never been universal in their scope and many, perhaps most, enactments of Parliament apply to special groups. Similarly, any attempt to use procedures as a criterion of the universality of law also fails, since these procedures change all the time. (For instance, correct observance of the relevant clauses of the *Mental Health Act* is a full legal answer to a writ of habeas corpus.[8]) In fact the universality implicit in the notion of the rule of law is purely formal. Its only universal feature is the definition of citizens as individual subjects of legal rights. And for this reason the law cannot represent a universality more substantive than that of society itself. All it does in the last analysis is confirm the rights of property.

Even when it is apparently providing real or specific justice for deprived groups in society, the state always maintains the legal form, and its justice is always formal. A clear example is the legislation to promote equal pay for women in industry. The tribunals created by this legislation treat women as a series of individuals, each the subject of a formal right to equal pay. But the concrete means for establishing the equality of female to male labour, a comparison required by the law, are conspicuously absent, and there is no provision for dealing with concentrations of female labour in a limited range of low-pay occupations. Because the law is formal it can easily be misinterpreted as a set of rules to be changed at will. It is tempting to see it as a frame which can hold any picture. Those views of the law which see it variously as a form of legitimacy or a code of violence fall into this error. The formal nature of the law, however, does not mean that the law is content-less: relations in society are only mediated through the legal form when appropriation occurs through private property, which is the implied content of all laws. Laws in capitalist society are a particular means of restructuring rational activity into capital and labour on an orderly basis. But this basis is not established in a once-and-for-all manner and the law has to be continuously modified, as social production evolves and the struggle of labour and capital develops. It is through this evolution brought about by the inadequacy of existing forms to changing conditions – an evolution which necessarily starts from the basis of existing forms – that the state renews itself and refurbishes its institutions to contain the evolution of social production. Formality has the possibility of elaboration but not the capacity to set itself in motion. The movement always comes from labour and, in this light, the evolution of law and administration originates with the development of social labour. Legal and administrative forms therefore always arise from the movements of labour and the efforts of the state to contain them in formal terms, so that the study of law and administration over time can be taken as an archaeology of decayed bodies politic, the corpses of organised working-class oppositions. The word 'administration' originates in seventeenth-century legal codes for the management of the estates of deceased persons, and modern administrative practices keep this etymology alive. Administration is working-class power *post festum*; working-class political victories captured and formalised at their moment of triumph. Thus, many of the bureaucracies and tribunals which impinge on the everyday life of the working class are the remains of famous political reforms of the past. The development of administration and the advance of technology both appear in the same light, as rationalisations which unfold themselves, each movement forward seeming to arise from a logical development of the previous one, but in both cases the appearance is false. In capitalist society technology has always developed in response to specific conditions as a means of overcoming working-class opposition to existing methods of production, and in this sense, of being precipitated by working-class struggles, new techniques can be seen as their obituary. So it is with administration, as every innovation, new body, tribunal or commission originates either directly or at one remove from working-class resistance to the formal conditions of its life. Just as machinery is the product of labour which then confronts its producer as an alien force, so administration is the appropriation of revolutionary will by the state, and its transformation into counter-revolutionary force.

Before the creation of the modern bureaucracies, an imperial administration had come into existence in England. The executive was purged of elements of mercantile specificity (Old Corruption) at the end of the eighteenth century, and administration was separated from politics institutionally, thereby allowing it room for manoeuvre. It was then reformed when the Liberals gained control of Parliament in the 1830s, after which came a rapid proliferation of departments of state, many of them based on the work of peripatetic inspectors. The outlook of liberal reform was an ethos of social policy, an amalgam of traditional concepts of order with a radical philosophical yearning for institutional streamlining. An emerging urban gentry, striving to identify their careers with the stability of bourgeois property, eagerly embraced this ethos. By the 1870s this new structure ossified into routine quite inadequate for the conditions it confronted, and a second period of liberal reform and state-building was begun. The administrative machine, once proliferated and given room for manoeuvre through its separation from politics, tended to reconstruct itself according to the imperatives of the real power at its command, and to throw up its own unconstitutional head. Edwin Chadwick made a determined bid to place himself at the head of the skeletal bureaucratic machine already in existence by the later 1840s. In 1919 a Treasury Minute vested authority over the whole state machine in a Treasury official, polemically nicknamed 'Master of the Offices', who appeared to be able to intervene even in defence matters. Formally, of course, the Crown (the Queen in Parliament) heads the executive, and not Parliament.

THE ELEMENTS OF PROPERTY

The elementary form of private property in law is *persona-res*[9] – a fragmentary derivation of a larger and more formally complete structure. The pivot of this structure, contract, has always been recognised by liberal theorists as the basic institution of civil society.

The first evidence of the enforceability of contracts is to be found in the second half of the fifteenth century, and the modern concept of contract was formulated by the middle of the sixteenth, coincident with the beginnings of wage labour. These developments which have never been codified in Britain, are referred to as 'common law'; their commonness deriving from the efforts of the late feudal monarchs to establish a set of administrative procedures which applied to all. The King's Peace meant that the King had universal jurisdiction (in contradistinction to the partial juridictions typical of feudalism), expressed in his Writ, addressed to his Officer, sitting in Court, with a Jury, to provide local knowledge and political grounding. These procedures were subsequently formalised into the legal system where they appeared as separate from the executive arm of the state – the so-called independence of the judiciary. However, this separation is only apparent; and there is no real distinction between law and administration. The remarkable growth of administrative law in recent years has effected a unity in practice that has been denied in constitutional theory.

While freedom of contract was one of the showpieces of the liberal epoch, it was never absolute, even formally. The state was never simply the third party to contract in the way that liberal theory fondly imagined in the late nineteenth century. From the earliest days of the common law in England, legal forms, such as contract, were supplemented by the law of Equity in the Chancery courts, where the Lord Chancellor could dispense a justice, which while legal, was not contained within the rigid procedures (real actions) of the common law. 'Equality is Equity' is an ancient English legal dictum which points to one basis on which the Lord Chancellor could modify contracts already entered. Even in the hey-day of so-called *laissez-faire*, the content of contracts was modified by statute, and in our own day they have been so structured, not only by statute law, but also by powerful collectivities, such as insurance companies when drafting their policies, that some would go so far as to say they have been destroyed.

The evolution of monarchical rule into law created a new professional caste of lawyers whose original problem, in this context, was to find a legal form adequate for the reciprocal private promises which comprise exchange. Their solution, the modern law of contract, is marked by its simplicity as a perfectly bilateral and consensual arrangement in which the binding element is mere agreement, rather than delivery of the object. They had to hand two well-developed legal forms, which at first sight appear ideal for the purpose, but these were too deeply rooted in the feudal conception of property.

(1) *Contract Re*: this was the legal framework for enforcing a transaction, part of which had already been carried out. Thus it was rooted in the specifics of the transaction in process. From this older law of actual transfer, the new law was to abstract legal personalities and their intentions of future performance. The feudal contract did not imply universal subjectivity and so was inadequate for absolute property. It did not see the citizen

as a property owner outside the possession of particular pieces of property.[10]

(2) *Covenant*: this involved a written commitment made under seal to pay, in money or in kind, for goods to be received. Whether the goods were actually received was irrelevant to the performance of the Covenant, which was an absolute commitment to make the transfer. It was a unilateral and public act, so that two parallel Covenants would be necessary to provide a sound guarantee at law for exchange. The shortcoming of this procedure for a law of absolute property was that it involved an intrusion of the state into the sphere of exchange that was too direct and visible to sustain the illusion of apparently spontaneous and reciprocal private promises.

A solution was found in the less obviously relevant delictual framework of the trespass laws, whereby a breach of 'contract' was converted into a tort, enabling the claimant to obtain damages for non-performance, just as he might for damage done through trespass. Known as *Assumpsit*, this law of trespass already foreshadowed modern contract by transforming particular transactions into relations between subjects set in a framework of absolute moral commitment. This effected a significant shift from the piecemeal character of legal transactions in the feudal period to the general mutuality of contract in the modern period, which is so removed from its rational basis that it has made the promise and its procedures sufficient basis for reciprocal legal obligation.

An important part of the legal structure of contract was the Doctrine of Consideration. If a person broke a contract, it was necessary to show objectively, i.e. in real terms specific to the case in hand, that he was committed to reciprocate. This was necessary since no general commitment to reciprocity existed prior to the legal birth of universal subjectivity. By the second half of the eighteenth century, Lord Mansfield was handing down judgements which attempted to substitute the idea of moral obligation for consideration, on the grounds that where there existed a legal or equitable obligation, the law should imply a promise, though none was ever made.[11] Here we see the modern individual in the process of construction, as the moral obligation to reciprocate is read into him by the state; thus the dictum: 'contract makes law'. Contrary to liberal theory, exchange and contract do not arise spontaneously in specific circumstances from relations between persons and things,

and through the judgements of Lord Mansfield the state produced
in the doctrine and practice of contract an appropriately mediated
social form. The complication, however, is that this form appears as
something other than what it really is. As it is formulated in terms of
persona-res, which appears to stand on its own for each individual
transaction, it does not appear social at all. The bourgeois contract
thus came to present itself in a feudal form, as though property
really were a relationship between a particular person and a specific
thing. Although the development of the modern doctrine of
contract represents a sharp rupture from the feudal past at one level,
its orgins in the feudal law of the King's Peace are unmistakable,
and the free individual of modern society retains the stigmata of his
servile past.[12]

A second way in which the law of trespass was used to found the
legal form of private property was in the law of theft. The turning-
point in legal doctrine came in 1473 with the Carrier's Case, which
established the misappropriation of an object as an act against the
state (violation of the King's Peace) and not just a civil wrong. Wool
belonging to an Italian merchant with a safe passage from the King
was seized by the carrier hired to transport it. This was not self-
evidently a felony because according to previous practice the carrier
argued that he had not taken by force, and hence against the Peace,
that which he already had in his possession. He was liable in the civil
courts, but the novel feature of the decision in his case was that he
was also found guilty of committing a trespass, which until then had
implied the physical removal of goods (rustling cattle being a
common example). This verdict was decisive for the formation of
modern law in that it first, separated the right of property from
direct possession; and second, made any transgression of this right
an act against the state, i.e. a crime. The evolution of the laws of
contract and theft completed the development of absolute
property – the absolute independence of property from specific
items (universal subjectivity).

It is obvious that the modern law of property was not established
overnight by a few acts of the late feudal monarch. This could not
have been the case, because in modern society the law of property
has to deal not only with finished products, but with the three
'factors of production': land, capital and labour. In each case the
general form *persona-res* has been elaborated.

The landed estate in the eighteenth century was the political-
economic base of a capitalised aristocracy, which received ground-

rent from tenant farmers, active capitalists, who advanced capital and employed wage labour. To preserve their class identity in the new society, the landowners had to bring their land into the sphere of private property while observing the estate as an entity, so as to prevent its dispersal to tenants. For this purpose they needed a legal form of property somewhat different from the contract, and the lawyers were naturally pleased to develop this for their patrons by means of the Doctrine of Estates. Between the land itself and the individuals who exercised control over it and enjoyed its rent, an elaborate abstraction was inserted, known as the Estate at Law. This included a concept of time, known in law as 'perpetuities', whereby an indefinite succession of future interests in the land, determined according to complex rules of inheritance and marriage settlement, were given a current market value – a sort of fourth dimension where future time existed in the present as a right. Ownership was then attached to these abstract entities, the succession of legal estates. In the Doctrine of Estates the authority to act (management) and proprietary right (use or enjoyment) were legally distinguished. Although this doctrine constituted a curious feudal relic in the epoch of modern property, the separation of control from ownership into two distinct legal categories fore-shadowed a crucial distinction in the legal form of capital established a century later.

In so far as the elementary form of property is adequate to the alienation of commodities within a framework of individual desire and consumption, so it proved adequate for the first phase of capitalist development when the process of accumulation was realised through the will of individual entrepreneurs. But as capital distinguished itself from simple property in the industrial revolution, this form, which had proved so effective in destroying feudal specificity, became a fetter on accumulation. The emergence of a new form adequate to capital as such, was delayed during the nineteenth century, lest it provide a basis on which the great mercantile monopolies of the eighteenth century could re-establish themselves. These large blocks of mercantile capital stood in opposition to the new industrialism and the expansion of production. Thus it was not until the old mercantile class and its ally, the landed aristocracy, which was fighting its own rear-guard action, had been politically defeated through the *Reform Act* of 1832, the *Poor Law Amendment Act* of 1834 and the *Repeal of the Corn Laws* in 1846, that pressure for the reform of capital ownership fully asserted itself as a demand for the legalisation of joint stock companies with limited liability.[13] Legislation in 1855 and 1862 established the principle of limited liability, which was consolidated in the 1880s with the development of an effective system of liquidation. One effect of the creation of this new legal form, which established a clear distinction between the private property of the capitalist (subject to consumption) and the property of the capitalist project (subject to accumulation), was the amalgamations of the 1890s. Its long-term result was the modern corporation, which now dominates every sector of the world economy.

Characteristically every capital now has many owners whose liabilities are limited to their investments, and cannot affect the rest of their property. At the same time, capital is administered by a corporate bureaucracy. Globalisation and diversification have led to the emergence of a general staff – a group of personnel specific to the accumulation process, whose members are not subjects of the property they control in the sense specified in the elementary legal form.[14] This form is now virtually extinct in the sphere of production and survives only for appropriating items of personal consumption. The point of the corporate form is not some as-sumed ideological function of making capitalists invisible and obscuring the nature of their property; it is capital's proper legal form.

As the elementary legal form was unable to contain the expanding force of social capital, new techniques outside the old common law procedures were developed. The common law itself evolved from the procedures of a central administration established by the Tudors in the process of disarming the feudal nobility (royal universalisation of jurisdiction). In this period of transition the feudal orders collapsed as civil or class society replaced them. In its completed form, class society comprised a series of individuals constituted as singularities or particular interests and consciences, and as the universal subjects of private property, over which they claimed absolute control.[15] In a word, this new society became a population. To crystallise the third factor of production, labour, out of the population required its own special property form , which has proved the most difficult of all to construct. The difficulty is that it has not only to provide a functioning framework within which, labour-power is bought and sold, but at the same time obscure the real nature of the transaction taking place.

THE WIDER LAW OF LABOUR

There are two senses of the concept of law. One relates to the legal system of the state; the second summarises the systematic behaviour of natural phenomena, i.e. the law of gravity. But they are not as unconnected as they appear at first sight. Social relations take the form of legal relations in capitalist society, because the movements of this society, its development and changes, are ones which can only be systematically grasped through the notion of law. This was more explicit in the nineteenth century, when a whole catalogue of social laws were produced: the survival of the fittest; the iron law of wages; diminishing marginal returns; and, definitively, the law of value. The legal system is an expression of the law-like nature of society, which is most clear in the case of labour. The detail law of labour, which is explicitly enacted by the state, derives from a *wider law of labour* that used to be known as the Poor Law.

Before wage labour became general, and the reserve army of paupers had been established as an integral aspect of the labour market itself, subsistence and employment were organised through the Poor Law. This was the law of labour in the widest sense, a law which regulated the internal relations of the poor by dealing with such problems as marriage break-up and illegitimacy. Parishes were required under the Old Poor Law to levy a rate for the maintenance of the poor and appoint overseers to allocate the funds. Justices of the Peace were given responsibility for this task and their powers included the regulation of wages and prices (these powers fell into disuse), as well as the implementation of the criminal law. The laws specifying the duties of the Justices of the Peace were the administrative law of the time, used later to specify the powers of the central executive. Enormous diversity was to be found in the ways in which these duties were implemented: boarding out was paid for; pensions granted; housing, fuel, clothing, medicine and funerals were provided. Many of the old workhouses became poorhouses, providing co-operative homes for the poor without supervision. Behind this mercantile diversity,[16] however, lay an essential structure; the organisation of conditions of subsistence through which the surplus population was determined and fashioned into a labour force.

The first experiments in the modern consumption of labour-power were pioneered by the authorities in houses of correction, where inmates were compelled to work in a disciplined way to produce a profit. But by the late eighteenth century the Poor Law authorities were dispensing relief to workers in their own homes (outdoor relief), because the intramural sphere of production had been taken over by capital in its factories; i.e. industry had become private. At this time (the last quarter of the eighteenth century) the wage had not yet emerged as a form of subsistence sharply differentiated from all others, and the majority of workers were still not entirely dependent upon a simple money wage. Poor Law outdoor relief, according to the number of children of the worker concerned and the current price of bread, was used to subsidise wages – for example, in the 1790s the Speenhamland system was established in some rural counties where underemployment was endemic.

Some parishes set a price for labour and levied a labour rate to bridge the gap between actual wages and this price; some compensated employers for the unavailability of labour; others allocated available work, each street taking its turn to have jobs (known as the roundsman system). There were many cases of parishes setting paupers up in trade, so taking them out of the labour market altogether. The payment of allowances was clearly the most attractive alternative for employers because, other things being equal, the higher they were, the lower could be wages. Finally, the 'law of settlement' constituted each parish as a local and self-contained labour market. This was the law which limited the right to relief to the parish of origin and no other.[17] Parishes tried to prevent people settling within their boundaries lest they might establish the right to relief for themselves and their children. They also used marriage and apprenticeship to get people out by creating the right to relief elsewhere. The discontinuities of these mercantile institutions meant that some people were temporarily or permanently outside the system, as parishes engaged in perpetual legal warfare to shift responsibilities.

The notorious 1834 *Poor Law Amendment Act*, which attempted to reform the Old Poor Law, was the watershed in the development of the wider law of labour. Marx attacked it as the creation of a Ministry of Pauperism, whose task was to administer and preserve bourgeois poverty. The Act contained three elements; (1) the central control of relief through new political institutions; (2) an attempt to limit outdoor relief to people unable to work; and (3) the restructuring of the workhouse into an instrument of administrative classification. In practice it took thirty to forty years to implement the Act because it met considerable resistance. On the other hand, certain urban parishes had been operating according to its principles for decades. The aim of abolishing 'indiscriminate' outdoor relief had long been canvassed by political economists and utilitarians. Malthus, for instance, had argued that the Poor Laws were incompatible with the institution of private property, and so should be completely abolished; and although this line of argument was dogmatically attractive to many intellectuals, it was not practical, since it failed to recognise the necessity for the legal regulation and administration of subsistence conditions for the proletariat, i.e. the wider law of labour. The predominance of outdoor relief was only significantly reduced in the 1870s, when the monetary alternative to the wage for the able-bodied was at last brought under control, and a clear administrative distinction made between wage and non-wage. Legislation abolishing truck and preferential interest rates on workers' savings helped to consolidate this separation. The 'impotent' poor (crippled, aged, mentally subnormal, etc.) remained in the classificatory workhouse at one remove from the logic of wage labour. This achievement of the administrative establishment of the wage as the normal form of subsistence for free labour involved the mobilisation of privately organised charity on a large scale. The Charity Organisation Society was formed in 1869 to rationalise private charity on behalf of the New Poor Law. It ironed out charity overlaps at the local level, and introduced systematic casework to prevent abuse and organise help into morally desirable channels.

Since this consolidation of the wage-form was not achieved until the 1870s, the importance of the 1834 *Poor Law Amendment Act*, and other reforms of the period, seems in some doubt. But their significance lay not in immediate changes of practice, but in establishing new political forms and administrative structures at central and local level to break with those developed by the mercantile gentry. The constitution of these political-administrative forms anticipated the development of their content – wage labour and the wage: but on the other hand they were a condition of its development. Hence the delay in implementation. In the case of the Poor Law these forms were: at the *local* level, a new unit of administration (the Union of Parishes) with an *elected* tax-raising body to control relief (Boards of Guardians) and to replace the magistracy.[18] This was a clear case of the liberal use of the vote as an instrument of state-building. At the *central* level the political innovation was even more dramatic. A collegiate board, the Poor Law Commission, was created: independent of direct Parliamentary or ministerial control, and working through peripatetic inspectors, its task was to bring the parishes in line with the new policy through a mixture of threat and persuasion. For a long time the commissioners remained content with purely verbal compliance. Any number of exceptions to favoured practice were accepted, so long as the parishes agreed in writing that they were indeed exceptions. But in the 1860s and 1870s the Commission (by then called a Board) began to impose the new system of classification and to contain outdoor relief.

The Commission itself was quite as revolutionary in terms of the innovation of political instrumentalities and liberal state-building as the policies it implemented. In some ways it can be argued that the constitution of the Commission was of even greater significance than its policies, since it consolidated the unitary structure of the state at one of its most vital points, namely the control of labour. Prior to the 1834 reform the organisation of relief through the parishes had been subject to only the loosest form of centralised control, with the result that the roots of political power were left largely untouched in the hands of the gentry as represented in the magistracy. More than any other measure, the New Poor Law consolidated the unitary structure of the political state in Britain, and it is no accident that this development occurred with respect to the control of labour, for in the last analysis, it is against labour that this unitary structure is ranged. The scale of the constitutional innovation was reflected in the scope of action of the new Commission, which was an elementary universal agency of administration, with great freedom of action, and ready to undertake almost any function: building bridges; providing medical services; shipping pauper children *en bloc* to northern factories.

In 1847 the Poor Law Commission was replaced by a ministry (confusingly named a Board), but the basic tendency persisted with the creation of many new boards at a distance from Parliament. Nassau Senior, an influential political economist, claimed this aspect of the Poor Law Amendment Act to have been a heavier blow to the aristocracy than the Reform Act itself. Where the latter broadened Parliament and narrowed the political base of the mercantile gentry, the former established a new local political form, the elected Board of Guardians, loosely linked by inspection to the central administrative agency, that by-passed the magistracy, and undercut its political roots. As regards its specific policies the New Poor Law created a structure for the administration of labour on the principle of classification. The Commissioners consistently promoted the construction of their new-style classificatory workhouses designed to replace the apparently chaotic ones of the mercantile epoch. Parishes were obliged to combine in the construction of these large purpose-built workhouses, within which an effort was made to segregate the elderly, the young, the sick, the insane, and the ablebodied. In so far as such classification destroyed localism and introduced specialists, it provided a substantive means for the growth of unitary state power. A whole series of institutions proliferated out of the classificatory workhouse in a way they could never have done out of the mercantile one: schools; dispensaries; infirmaries; lunatic asylums; reformatories; old-age homes; subnormality hospitals. Each sphere spawned a body of experts, professionals closely integrated into the state.

Classification laid the groundwork for the administrative rationalisation of the labour market. In the New Poor Law an absolute distinction was attempted between poor labourers and destitute paupers, i.e. the unemployed, who were not yet classified as such by the state. This distinction was organised in terms of the character of the pauper: his demoralisation (loss of morality). A transitional category which emerged three-quarters of the way through the nineteenth century was the 'residuum', referring to that section of an overstocked labour market whose pathological incapacity for rational action, and consequent unemployability, was thought to be both genetically and environmentally determined. The residuum was a transitional category in the sense that it was not seen as the very lowest level of society, but as a stratum in the lower reaches that did in fact have one foot in the labour market but was unable to take the second step signifying its full inclusion. Thus it could be suggested in the 1890s that the stratum be bodily removed from the London labour market to labour colonies at home or colonies abroad. Finally, in the 1890s, these various distinctions gave way to the principle of continuity along the employed–unemployed axis, embracing the whole of society, and fulfilling population as a category.

The first global reference to employed manual workers appeared in official documents in 1887, before which time all the relevant trades of the workers under discussion were solemnly listed one by one. Unemployment as an administrative category emerged a little later, having been introduced into the language of political economy a short time before by Alfred Marshall. The word itself had of course been used over the centuries, and more specifically in Owenite debates earlier in the century. From the 1890s heated debates occurred as to its causes: Hobson attributed it to under-consumption; Pigou to the failure of wages to adjust to the demand for labour; Keynes integrated both these interpretations into his *General Theory*; but here the so-called causes of unemployment do not concern us, only its emergence as a category of state administration. Whereas the Poor Law provided for the ad-ministrative regulation of those outside the labour contract, the potential inclusion of the poor into the labour force through the category of unemployment led to the direct regulation of the whole population. The Poor Law fostered an ontology of poverty, where the pauper was one of a series of discrete types, and could be more or less permanently deposited in one of a series of institutions. *With unemployment, every worker became a potential pauper.*

We are talking here of developments in the late nineteenth century when wage labour had become the general form of appropriation for the working class, or, to say the same thing, the whole class had notice of poverty served upon it. In this situation residual specificities in the administration of poverty had to be discarded, and in their place new general practices of insurance established on a fiscal basis. While administration always takes place through specific categories, the important thing from this time on was that these categories were derived from a unitary basis. The first group to be insured in this way were workers quite unlike the traditional image of the pauper: the skilled. Those, like the Webbs, who were still in 1909 trying to perpetuate the ontology of poverty in a rationalised system of state confinement of the recalcitrant, were simply by-passed by the new political-administrative forms of the Liberal programme of 1906–11. Although this programme included a non-contributory old-age pension scheme, initially with certain behavioural (ontological) requirements determining eligibility, we can take the *National Insurance Act* (1911), Parts I and II, as the *locus classicus* of the wider law of labour and, indeed, the modern state-form. Part I of the Act covered health; Part II, unemployment.

Flat-rate contributions, symbolised by the insurance stamp, embodied individual thrift and personal property right, at the same time as they broadened the national tax base (contributions being payable by many who normally paid no tax), and put money into the pockets of the unemployed.[19] The practices initiated by the Act subsumed aspects of the intense class struggles taking place at that time, into a gigantic structure of administration and quasi-judicial tribunals, established in every region of the country. Although it was a government insurance scheme, it was in part privately administered in order to conciliate various vested interests. In the early years of the Act there was a continual movement of individuals into and out of insurance, which was still far from universal, its scope being determined by income and contract of service. The universalisation of social insurance was finally proposed in the Beveridge Report of 1942. Part I of the 1911 *National Insurance Act*, which covered health, provided for free medical care by the GP, plus ten shillings a week for twenty-six weeks and five shillings a week thereafter. Initially the scheme involved five-sixths of the families in the United Kingdom, although many individuals within those families were excluded from it.

The moral imperative of the Poor Law was carried over into the new legislation, which reinforced the obligation to work through a system of personal enquiry; upheld certain family obligations; and reprehended the criminal pauper. But the same trend which was already expressing itself in the franchise, equality before the law, manifested itself in the field of labour. The *Workmen's Compensation Act* of 1897 is an example of this. The Act granted a right to compensation for personal injury by accident at work, thus by-passing the common law action of Negligence. Moves had already been made in this direction in 1880 with the *Employers' Liability Act*, which abolished the defence of Common Employment in certain Negligence actions. Common Employment meant that the worker was assumed to have accepted the risks arising from the carelessness of his fellow workers. This legislation established a new site for an old struggle over malingering: was the worker shamming, or was the apparent malfunction genuine? To determine the point a whole branch of medicine was developed by doctors working for the insurance companies who covered the employers' risks under the Compensation Acts. A start had already been made on this para-medical doctrine in the armed forced and penal institutions of the eighteenth century, and in legal practices concerning criminal responsibility.

It has been estimated by B. Gilbert that from 1921–7 nearly one half of all working-class households were using the National Health Insurance sickness or disablement benefit as a supplement for income. In 1927 nearly one half of married women drew the sickness and/or disablement benefit.[20] In the Depression, what appeared to the working class as a possibility of subsistence, appeared to the state as malingering, and the claim was made that not all those women were genuinely ill. It was pointed out that married women continued to do housework although officially ill, which made it impossible to apply a test of sickness. Doctors at the time had little alternative but to sign certificates if they wished to retain their clientele. In the end centrally controlled state medical officers were used to check certificates, and many were discountenanced. To combat this so-called malingering, Sir John Collie, the chief medical expert on compensation, advised doctors not to live too near their working-class patients, lest they be unduly influenced by their way of thinking.[21]

For the unemployed on the dole, restrictions were organised through the *Genuinely Seeking Work* rule. In areas of massive unemployment, claimants in the 1920s were required to prove that they had been genuinely seeking work, by producing bus tickets or other proof of visits to factories. Official committees sent out 'spies' to question a man's neighbours as to whether he was idle and feckless, and many claims were disallowed on the basis of character assessments acquired this way. Although the category of unemployment that formed the basis of the *National Insurance Act* pushed to one side the historic division of the working class into the employed on the one hand, and the pauper on the other hand, it did not emancipate the working class from wage labour, but simply served notice of poverty upon the whole class. In other words, the advent of unemployment declared the absolute poverty of the working class in a clear and unmistakable fashion, in return for which it was admitted to the franchise as full members of the state.

THE LABOUR CONTRACT

Every law enacted by the state in respect of labour is forced to be consistent with a law given to the state, over which it exercises no authority itself. This is the law of value which decrees the proletariat, whose general conditions of existence have to be regulated through the state by the wider law of labour. This law includes both the organisation of the reserve army and the general determination of the proletariat as a class by such means as the police. Within the wider law of labour the state has to formulate a narrow law directed towards the determination of the labour contract through which workers and capital meet directly.

Labour law is the most complex and equivocal of the laws of property for fundamental reasons. All empirical laws of capitalist society derive ultimately from the law-like nature of this society, although this is not directly visible in them. Thus actual contracts of employment embody what can be called a *labour contract* which formalises conditions necessary for labour-power to be sold as a commodity. The buying and selling of labour-power summarises the contradictions of capitalist society in a single moment. The impossibility of formulating a contract of employment according to the general principles of the formation of contracts originates here.

The overriding importance of this labour contract has never been theoretically recognised by jurists, even those working in the Marxist tradition who were particularly sensitive to the problems of labour. E. B. Pashukanis, when developing his categories of legal subject and legal object, wrote at the time of the restoration of the contract of employment in the Soviet Union. But he did not discuss this branch of the law, except to say in passing, that relations of dominance and subservience in industry flow directly from the conditions of production (economic forces, dead matter), and are therefore incomprehensible to jurists. Because the authority of the capitalist, unlike that of the controllers of slaves or serfs, was 'not theoretically or politically established', it did not have to be juridically privileged. The establishment of labour regulations was therefore always an act of private legislation, dressed up in the fiction of contract.[22]

Karl Renner, the Austro-Marxist jurist, recognised that the employment contract was one without contractual content; its content being command. This contract, an alliance with the law of property, produced an organisation similar to the state: the power hierarchy of factory production. Renner's discussion of the labour contract had the merit of being rooted in a broad concept of a legal order of labour. As the historical rise of private property destroyed the economic substratum of family law, it was replaced by poor laws and social legislation. Subsistence and social reproduction were thus guaranteed; at the same time, the family became a point of intersection for individual lives linked to various centres of authority (i.e. various schools and factories). Just as Pashukanis felt the regulation of labour must elude jurists, so Renner thought the ability of the capitalist to plan his factory organisation was a right that had been added inconspicuously to his personal, absolute domination over a corporal thing of elementary property. The form remained and persisted, while the social content had changed. The machine was substituted for paternal and conjugal power.[23]

Both these writers made the error of grasping authority over labour as delegated public authority; a structure analogous, or complementary, to the institution of private property. A brick (contract) was taken out of one edifice (property) and put into another (the order of labour). Renner argued that since the right of personal freedom is the negation of labour control (repeal of combination acts, wages' regulation, etc.), the ownership of a person in his labour-power is not in any sense a property right. For him the legal definition of wage labour is *do ut facias*: I pay, you work. It is not *persona-res*, as in the elementary property form. Thus the law of labour must be a code of regulation, and is not integral to private property. Here we have one of the most important of the modernist separations: economic conditions are separated from the state, but strangely give rise to a power structure analogous to that of the state.

All subsequent critiques of the law of labour contracts follow the same lines. O. Kahn Freund writes: 'The main object of labour law has always been, and I venture to say will always be, to be a countervailing force to counteract the inequality of bargaining power which is inherent and must be inherent in the employment relationship. . . . It is an attempt to infuse law into a relation of command and subordination.'[24] In common with the two Marxist jurists, he failed to recognise that the law (and the state) must already be there. The formal freedom of modern society necessitates a labour contract, so that labour-power can be sold as an object. And although this narrow law of labour can never be perfectly articulated by the jurist, it is the foundation of labour regulation.

Jurisprudence has recently rediscovered the 'structural problem' of the contract of employment which it now recognises 'has never been systematically articulated', though it fails to explain why this is the case.[25] Similarly sociologists point out that the contract of employment fails to deal with real relations of power: whether it be the power that management exercises over the worker or the power workers themselves enjoy by participating in management. But though sociology recognises the problems caused by 'theoretical inequality and hierarchy', like jurisprudence it does not grasp the issues at stake.[26]

A simple contrast of the buying and selling of labour-power with other commodities reveals the difficulty facing the legislator. When an individual sells a commodity other than labour-power, the act of sale is a final alienation. He parts with the object at the moment of making the agreement to sell, and the subsequent use of the object by the purchaser is a matter of indifference to him. This is not the case with labour-power, which is an attribute of the subject and cannot be consumed without his presence, participation and co-operation. Unlike other objects which are external to the seller, labour-power cannot be definitively alienated. Thus the first difficulty is to formulate a labour contract which provides for the alienation of an object – which by its very nature cannot be alienated. Or to put it another way, the difficulty is one of including labour-power within the general law of property, while at the same time being forced to acknowledge that labour-power is not an object of property like others.

The second difficulty of labour law, and a consequence of the first, is that the alienation of labour-power which actually occurs, and which the labour contract is there to effect, must in fact be denied by the contract, since it is incompatible with the general presuppositions of private property. If the labour contract were formulated in such a way as to recognise that the worker was actually alienating his capacities, it would be inconsistent with the general principles of the formation of contracts (consideration; privity; intent to enter legal relations). That is to say, it would be inconsistent with the definition of the worker as a universal subject in full possession of himself at all times. Philosophers in the seventeenth century were especially sensitive to this point, that wage labour was incompatible with freedom (private property) since the latter required the individual to retain precisely that which he alienated to his employer: his will and its rational use. The incompatibilities between the terms of wage labour and private property are so fundamental that labour law has never been fully included within the general law of property: historically it moved directly from the mercantile law of domestic service to modern administrative law. This objective contradiction in the legal situation should not be mistaken for a logical contradiction. Its

origins are anterior to law and appear as logical problems in its
formulation.

The solution that the law has developed combines two elements:

(1) The episodic nature of the transaction: so that the worker only
submits himself to capital period by period, and never finally
alienates his will. This permits the illusion that he remains in
ultimate possession of himself. Paradoxically the solution
appears as a problem to the jurist which he then solves by
reading continuity directly into the contract itself: 'Hence the
contract has a two-tiered structure. At the first level there is an
exchange of work and remuneration. At the second level there
is an exchange of mutual obligations for future performance.'[27]
(2) In the contract itself the object that is formally alienated does
not appear as labour-power, i.e. a capacity which is an
immediate attribute of the subject, but as labour, i.e. expended
labour-power, or labour which has become external to the
worker.

Once labour-power has been consumed and embodied in
products, it is no longer a personal capacity, but has been
transformed into a more orthodox type of object, which can be sold
without directly impugning the independent will of the subject.
Hence the labour contract specifies labour as its object, and the
worker is not formally paid the requirements of his subsistence, but
for the amount of work he performs. Thus, unlike other payments,
the wage is paid after the consumption of the commodity, and not
before, and then made dependent upon effective consumption.

One reason why jurists have been able to establish labour as the
object of contracts, and set to one side the question of subsistence, is
that the latter is organised through the wider law of labour. It would
appear that jurisprudence has not accepted the real relationship
between the wider and narrower law of labour, which it sees only in
formal terms of the classification of contracts of employment. In
industrial relations, breach of contract, which is part of the wider
law of labour, is defined in terms of employment contracts
themselves formulated in terms of the narrow law. The consequence
of this has been that the real requirements of subsistence, i.e. the
major task of the wider law of labour, are extruded outside the law
proper and handled administratively and fiscally. The wider law of
labour is concerned with the conditions of labour-power, and the

Poor Law in the nineteenth century like social insurance in the twentieth, acknowledged the necessity of subsistence. This left the way open for the narrow law of labour to ignore it altogether and substitute labour as the object in place of labour-power. Without the wider law of labour, rooted in subsistence, it would be impossible for the state to formulate the narrow law which goes as far as it does to reconcile the buying and selling of labour-power with the premises of universal subjectivity.

In composing the fully developed wage contract, it is necessary for the state to establish the subjectivities of both parties, since neither capital nor labour are spontaneous economic entities. In the case of the purchaser, this was relatively straightforward and was achieved first through the elementary legal form and subsequently through the joint stock company. In the case of the seller, the problem of establishing a formal subjectivity was more demanding. The necessity and even existence of such a subjectivity has always been shrouded in the powerful myth of voluntary collective bargaining, which gives the impression that working-class organisations exist spontaneously outside the law.[28] But, on the contrary, trades unions have from 1871 been the legally constituted subjectivity of the working class. Despite elements of class autonomy, they are creatures of the state in a deeper sense than their recent collaboration would suggest. Thus before we can approach the labour contract this myth must be dispelled. Contrary to the claim that collective bargaining takes place outside the law, the space in which working-class organisations operate has been defined by the state since the effective legalisation of unions. One ground for the myth that free collective bargaining lies outside the state is the belief that its results are not contracts at law. These results are not definitely constituted as formal contracts, and there were no judgements on the issue at all until 1971; nevertheless they are *de facto* contracts, known simply as collective agreements. The critical point is not the juridical status of these agreements, but the fact that they can only exist because the state has legalised trades unions and determined their constitutions. By participating in continual collective bargaining – continual because of not resulting in definitive legal agreements – the trades unions are simply engaging in administration. Mario Tronti has argued that where trades unions establish legally binding agreements for a period of years, this is an advance for the working class: the unions at least appear to cease to be administrators of labour law.[29] Even this is doubtful as it does not in itself check the control which unions exercise over their members. In fact unions have been encouraged in various countries to engage in contract bargaining precisely in order to strengthen control over their members. The attempt in Britain to formalise this control through legislation in the *Industrial Relations Act* (1971) proved a serious failure. It attempted to combat the unofficial strike and the local drift of wages up from an agreed national level with the legal concept of 'unfair industrial practice'. The Act was repealed within three years.

It is now possible to identify three phases in the development of the narrow law of labour:

(1) *The establishment of collective bargaining* (the period up to 1918): disputes between an employer and his employees in the eighteenth and throughout most of the nineteenth centuries came under the law of 'master and servant'. Based on a *contract of service*, it was assumed that the servant was subject to positive direction in his tasks by his master, who had proprietary rights in his service, so that if the servant were injured, it was the master who claimed compensation for loss of service. The elementary legal form of property, though it broke with this formulation at a much earlier date, had originally shared in it. If someone failed to complete an exchange, he was sued for failure to perform, analogously with the failure to perform a service. Contract broke with this in the sixteenth century, but sanctions against labour were deemed to be criminal, rather than civil, as late as the *Master and Servant Act* (1875). The logic of contracts of service derived from the working conditions of domestic servants and farm labourers who, prior to the industrial revolution, often lived in. The legal framework included more than a simple agreement to buy and sell labour. Although they were legalised in 1824, trades unions were not granted effective legal power to act until the *Trades Union Act* (1871), which protected them from the common law doctrine forbidding action 'in restraint of trade'. An Act of 1875 consolidated their position by eroding criminal liability for the consequences of industrial actions. This immunity from penal sanction was expressed in the 'golden formula' of 'acts in contemplation or furtherance of a trade dispute'. Civil liabilities remained, and in the 1890s the courts invented the tort of inducing a breach of contract (the Taff Vale case). This was swept away by the *Trade Disputes Act* (1906), which gave immunity from civil laws if the golden formula was observed, and relieved unions from liability for

the acts of their members. This Act has been the legal basis of trades union activity ever since, although the courts went on handing down hostile decisions until the end of the First World War, and hostile legislation was passed in 1927 after the General Strike. The *Rookes* v. *Barnard* case in the House of Lords in 1964 showed that the courts are still capable of further invention in this field.[30]

This sequence of legislation defining both labour organisations and their space in law, was the formation of the legal subjectivity of labour by the state. Alongside it, the state took various initiatives to regulate the labour market, such as protective legislation for women and children and the establishment of labour exchanges. The legalisation of trades unions was part of the transformation of the working class into an active subject of property. When the working class was recognised as a general force in society (a class), it was necessary to grant it the legal right to use force in relation to its labour: the right to strike. This was not of course expressed as such legally, but appeared negatively as inaction, as a series of immunities, which effected a legal breach of property forms other than labour, and so recognised the limits of the common law. Recent legislation has been concerned with reconstructing labour as a legal object so as to repair the breach in common law by narrowing the space between it and administrative law.

The recognition of the proletariat as the class subject of a general force marked a decisive moment in the development of the state and a clear break from the feudal past. Right was extended to all, and all discontinuities were overcome as the state addressed itself to all classes of society on the same terms. In a sense one can take this moment of the full legal recognition of working-class subjectivity as the completion of the development of the state into a unitary state. (2) *Parallel machinery* (1918–65): the law now proceeded to deal with specific categories of labour in order to strengthen this subjectivity. From the end of the First World War until recently courts rarely intervened in industrial disputes and unions believed themselves free from liability for economic torts. Picketing case law was so hard to find that legal text books had to use Irish examples. Statutory law was concerned to set up negotiating machinery parallel to that already developed in the better organised industries. Most of the important measures had been taken by the end of the First World War, by which time the framework for the next half century had been erected. From 1891 the state began to insist upon fair wages as a condition in some of its contracts with civil engineering firms. Mining and agricultural wages were dealt with by separate government departments, and minimum wage legislation in 1909 specified that negotiating machinery backed up by inspection, be set up in some low-pay areas. Arbitration machinery was created by the *Industrial Courts Act* (1919).

(3) *Re-composing a contract* (1965 to the present time): although threatening or inducing breaches of employment contracts became immune from civil suits in 1965, there has over the last twenty years been a movement towards the direct structuring of individual employment contracts. Legislation concerning their commencement and termination was passed: the *Terms and Conditions of Employment Act* (1959) compulsorily implied the terms of the contract of employment for an employee even where he had never seen the contract itself; and the *Contract of Employment Act* (1963) required new employees to be given a contract when they started work. At the other end, the *Redundancy Payments Act* (1965) specified recompense for redundancy. A system of industrial jurisprudence to handle disputes arising from this legislation has been established on the basis of tribunals originally set up to deal with a training levy on industry. The tendency in British legislation has been to compel employers to offer pay and conditions as if they had negotiated them, similar to the way in which Lord Mansfield's judgements implied a legal promise even where none had been made.

In the last twenty years there has been an unmistakable tendency towards legal formalisation of the employment contract. The underlying reason for this must undoubtedly be the increasing difficulties of managerial discipline in conditions of full employment. The difficulties in composing a contract of employment consistent with the premises of common law is only one side of the problem: the real difficulty which no contract, however well articulated, can ever overcome is the consumption of labour-power at the place of work. The efforts to fully articulate the employment contract, together with more elaborate systems of payment, such as measured day work, provide an index of the difficulties experienced by employers in this field.

It is through the law of labour in both its wider and narrower sense that the working class has been brought into the state and its sphere of right. In the nineteenth century, before the working class was a fully developed subject of right, industrial misconduct was dealt with through the criminal law and the civil law of tort; while the man lacking subsistence was designated a pauper and subjected to institutional regulation. After the First World War, with the extension of the sphere of right to the whole working class, the courts abstained from direct intervention in industrial disputes, while those without means were designated unemployed, and maintained within civil society by insurance or gratuitous payments.

It was only after the working class had become a subject of right that it was possible to formulate a modern employment contract. Or to look at it from the other point of view, a modern employment contract presupposes the working class as a subject of right. In this sense the narrow law of labour rests upon the wider law. Such are the peculiarities of labour-power as a commodity that the legal form of the contract governing its sale and purchase cannot state its real content. If the real content were made explicit, the contradiction between formal equivalence and real subsumption would be clear, and the inconsistency of the wage relation with the general form of property would be out in the open. Moreover, unlike other contracts, that which includes labour-power cannot even carry an aura of spontaneity, and from the first origins of wage labour in the modern period, the state has been compelled to take explicit responsibility for its construction.

The formal structure of the labour contract can be summarised under three headings:

(1) *The parties to the contract*: in exchange there must be formally independent parties. In labour law the state has to specify that the unions exist and that they are genuinely independent from the employers (i.e. not company unions). In other words, the state constitutes the parties as autonomous elements within the contract, and specifies whom they represent by setting up mechanisms for the representation of labour interests. In liberal society it does not establish trades unions directly but rather opens the space within which they exist and stipulates the processes through which they operate. For instance, rules are established for determining whether a union represents workers who are not its members. In the United Kingdom where the legal status of industrial agreements is open to question, it is not clear who the legal parties to an industrial agreement are: the unions, their agents, or the members?

(2) *Equivalence in the contract*: because English law leaves it open as to whether the bargainers actually conclude a contract at law, it is

obliged to treat their agreement as the content of myriad individual contracts of employment. Each of these has terms which were formerly defined by tradition ('reasonably certain and notorious custom'); then by the present conduct of the parties; and most recently by incorporation of collective agreements by reference to statute, such as the *Equal Pay Acts* and *Health and Safety at Work Act*. The point of substance behind these changing procedures is the attempt to give formal weight to managerial power by imposing upon the individual workers collectively agreed conditions of work. Thus the employer who was part of a national agreement with a union could claim that the national scope of the agreement applied to an individual worker, and attempt to legally impose its terms upon him personally. The courts have so far been unsympathetic to employers who have attempted to do this.

Although the content of the employment contract on the worker's side can be formally specified, it cannot be legally guaranteed: even when the state takes exceptional action to prohibit strikes, it cannot legislate the intensity of work.

(3) *The act of exchange itself*: free will is the essential element in the formal conditions of exchange, but the state has to determine this in the case of many workers, e.g. white-collar workers, without a strong tradition of organised opposition. Similarly, a duty to bargain may have to be imposed on employers, and facilities supplied for the actual process of bargaining. At the same time freedom of contract is negated by incomes policies and wage freezes.

Contrary to liberal thought, no contract is spontaneously created by its own parties, but all contracts are constructed through the state. In the case of the labour contract even the illusion of spontaneity is lacking. The reasons for this go right back to the ambiguous nature of labour-power as a commodity. Where two individuals exchange commodities other than labour-power, it is possible to conceive their contract as arising spontaneously from reciprocal needs; but where labour-power is sold, this is not possible. For the need to sell labour-power presupposes non-reciprocity between buyer and seller, since the former is the possessor of (real) property, while the life of the latter is defined entirely by its absence. And it is this absence, rather than spontaneous need, that precipitates him into exchange. The fundamental non-equivalence of the parties involved provides the real content of the labour contract, but one that is inconsistent with its formal terms of equivalence and freedom. The difficulties, therefore, of composing a labour contract that is consistent with the general laws of property, universal subjectivity and freedom, are therefore of a very fundamental nature.

The labour contract is part of the general law of property, but at the same time inconsistent with it. This becomes apparent in the right to strike, which is a presupposition of all labour contracts since it is directly rooted in the conditions of free labour. The wage relation has real and formal aspects: in the one, workers with no independent means of living submit themselves to the will of another; in the other, free individuals make contracts for the sale and purchase of a commodity like any other. The real conditions of the wage relation, therefore, are absolute poverty, alienation of self and submission; its formal conditions are rights and freedom. Their reconciliation, which is inevitably tense and precarious, is effected through two procedures: (1) the constitution of the wage as a payment for labour and not labour-power; and (2) the purchase and sale of labour-power on a periodic or episodic basis, so that the worker is left in formal possession of his capacities and therefore formal possession of himself, i.e. free. The right to strike is essentially a corollary of these fundamental procedures, since it confirms the freedom of the worker; or to put it the other way, without the right to strike the formal freedom of the worker would be seriously impugned, and with it the universality of private property.

The ambiguous legal status of agreements entered into by trades unions is also a necessary consequence of the fundamental conditions of the formal freedom of labour. As the legal subjectivity of labour has been collectivised with the development of production, the rights that attach to the individual worker have simply been extended, and trades union legislation, even where it has consciously sought to restrict the space in which workers can collectively exercise their rights, has always acknowledged and upheld the right to strike. This fact is decisive for the liberal state and marks it off from other political state-forms of this century – fascism, corporatism, communism. The concession of the right to strike together with the definition of the wage as a payment for labour, and the buying and selling of labour-power, upon a periodic basis, are procedures through which the real and formal conditions of wage labour are held in balance. But this balance does not resolve the contradiction; rather it holds it in check and at the same time gives rise to a whole series of ambiguities in the legal framework. The most dramatic of these concerns the right to strike, because this permits, explicitly within the framework of contract, the right of one party to break contract and create circumstances in which further employment contracts and commercial agreements are broken by other parties. The right to strike is a legal force which infringes the general law of property. Workers, individually and collectively, in the field of employment are the only subjects in capitalist society who are legally allowed to use force, i.e. to disregard contract, in pursuit of their own interests.

In so far as the right to strike allows a party to exercise force in pursuit of its own interest, it breaches the general character of right which disallows such a direct use of force. This is further evidence of the peculiar nature of labour-power as a legal object. Paradoxically, therefore, the generalisation of the property-form to include labour-power can only be achieved by immunities that permit breaches of contract. Suggestions that the right to strike be abridged on the grounds of national efficiency without undermining the whole legal apparatus of liberal democracy are simply facile.[31]

In Britain, unlike some other countries, the right to strike is not formally codified, but made effective through a series of immunities and specific provisions, ranging from social security payments to strikers' families, to the laws on picketing.

The recent *Employment Act* (1980) once again confirms the right of workers to strike (the golden formula), but at the same time attempts to confine the legal space within which it can be exercised: (1) it removes immunity from 'secondary' picketing, and from those breaches of commercial contract deemed remote from the original dispute; (2) it removes immunity for acts of 'coercive recruitment' of union members.

Following the Act a code of picketing has been introduced, but its purpose was admittedly educational and has so far only been legally invoked once. In 1979 a court decision widened the definition of a trade dispute, and led to the apparently more drastic legislation now being canvassed by the government. This would establish criteria for whether actions could be reasonably thought capable of furthering a trade dispute; and perhaps limit the concept of trade dispute itself to an action mainly or wholly related to a set of legally established ends or subjects. The Minister hints at a thorough-going reform of the law so that the right to strike would become a positive right in law on the one hand, and industrial agreements become enforceable contracts on the other. The former would require a whole range of subsidiary measures to mesh it in with existing property law; and these together with the second proposal would give unions greater power over their members.

Legislation of this sort appears drastic, and in a formal sense it is; but it has become necessary because of the intensification of the discrepancies between the real and formal subsumption of labour – the class struggle. In the end the impossibility of writing a perfect labour contract arises from the contradiction between its formal and real conditions. As the focus for class struggle, it leads to a series of shifts and manoeuvres. The narrow law of labour cannot be fitted into the general law of property, and even the various procedures that are developed to overcome this cannot in themselves achieve the real purpose of a labour contract, namely the guarantee that workers deliver specified amounts of labour to their employers. This impossibility defines the frontier of formality in capitalist society, and the starting-point for the generalised application of force to control the conditions of labour.

POLICE AND PUBLIC PROPRIETY

Enormous force is first of all present in the separation of the needs and capacities of labour so that they can only approach each other, as subjectivity and objectivity, through the mediation of capital. Since legal forms such as the employment contract cannot bolt these elements securely in place, force must be continuously applied to hold them together.

Subjectivity and objectivity are formally united in so far as a subject implies an object and an object a subject, and neither can stand alone: in reality, however, they repel each other. Subjectivity and objectivity attract each other like opposing magnetic poles, but when the subject is forced to take itself as object, and the real difference between them is obliterated, they repel each other like identical poles. It is this latter tendency which obliges the state to continually exercise force, since it is the repulsion of subjectivity and objectivity which emerges at the most strategic point in the whole edifice of private property. This is the definition of labour-power as a commodity, where subjectivity as the universal possibility of wealth directly. confronts objectivity as its complete absence. In order to guarantee the labour market the state must unceasingly apply force to prevent the tense unity that defines labour-power as a commodity from disintegrating.

Political society denies the future by refusing to contemplate even the possibility of a higher stage of history, and so misrepresents the contradictions of its own order which bear this possibility, as threats of a total breakdown of society into primal chaos. This mystifies reality, but only in passing. It is in the nature of the formality of the order out of which the state arises and which it then preserves by force, that the rational kernel of modern society, which carries the seed of an alternative future, is made invisible. The misrepresentation of contradictions as disorders is replicated in the conceptualisation of force as something apart from property. The order of capitalist society is invisible and political theorists have had to seek the principle of cohesion in a *deus ex machina*: in exactly the same way force, power and violence have been reintroduced into the action as the machinations of some offstage impressario.

Private property is a field of force, its presuppositions can only be established by force, and the contradictions which threaten to tear it apart, can only be held in check by force. Thus private property and its order, pulling itself apart and being riven together again all the time, is in a continual state of *tension*. The force which the state maintains as one element in this tension is fundamental for order. And the state brings it to bear through its ability to deploy the means of coercion. When these means of exercising force are structured into the property-form and citizenship, and deployed on a correspondingly formal basis, they take the recognisable form of political power.

Although violence was the midwife of private property, it does not directly accompany the routine functioning of circulation, and this lends plausibility to the widely held belief that the practice of force is something apart from the routine of daily life. By contrast to the feudal corvée where the compulsion to work was explicit, force appears notably absent from the buying and selling of labour-power. Strikes are the exception that prove the rule. Nevertheless force is always present, although not immediately visible.

(1) Historically, capitalist property came into the world covered in blood and dirt. In the phase of primitive accumulation the world was ransacked to transfer value to Europe. At the same time producers at home were subjected to a long, drawn-out

process of expropriation, managed through savage penality on the one hand, and the Poor Law as a police measure on the other, which turned them into a proletariat.

(2) A branch of the social division of labour exists alongside production devoted exclusively to the exercise of the means of coercion. Its specialisation as part of the division of labour gives rise to the illusion that it is abstracted from the social matrix, and that the force which it exercises originates apart from property. Sovereignty then appears both autonomous and fragmented into various powers.

Until the turn of this century, liberal political theory acknowledged the all-pervasive and constitutive nature of force. The force which saturated political institutions and its subjective correlate, pain, were considered crucial to the integrity of the state. Fitzjames Stephen, the nineteenth-century judge, for instance, developed concepts of punishment and reconstructed legal codes on this theme.

Force in capitalist society, and its formal constitution as political power, is always directed back to maintaining the chasm between needs and capacities, and holding in place the bond through which they approach each other as subjectivity and objectivity. To put it another way, it always acts directly or indirectly on the conditions that separate labour-power on the one side, from the activity and products of labour on the other. Thus labour-power cannot be realised directly, but must be sold as a commodity, and it is through the payment for this sale, the wage, that needs are appropriated on the other side. Thus between capacities and needs stands capital. But while capital stands as a wedge that fragments the real unity of labour, labour is no less a wedge which sunders the formal unity of capital. Thus the movement of value from money to money, which is the character of capital, can never be direct or unmediated, for capital-in-general. It always has to interrupt itself by purchasing and consuming labour-power and it then depends for the reflux of money, at least in part, upon the workers' spending their wages. Thus capitalist society presents a doubly contradictory picture of two processes: those of labour and capital, which simultaneously split each other apart and tie each other together. The extreme tension under which this precarious unity (reproduction) is held together, determines both the necessity for force and its nature.

In separating capacities from needs and mediating them through money, capital robs labour of particularity and constructs labour-power as a general force or activity. In other words, it denies labour the grounds of rationality and creates it as undifferentiated general force – labour-power is simply the capacity to work. But while this general force can only be brought about by a power as general as itself, i.e. the absolute sovereignty of the state, at the same time, since the general cannot exist immediately in its own right, but only in the form of particularities, not only must labour-power be purchased through individual workers, but the state can only exercise its sovereignty through a series of specific forces.

The fear that the forerunners of the proletariat in the sixteenth century would invade property gave birth to the 'science of police', which consisted of a rationalisation of the powers of the new central authority to impose order, and the means through which this was to be achieved. However, the contingency of means was not recognised by this science, in the sense that it did not separate them from ends. And so its most significant feature was the all-encompassing definition of its goals: it was concerned not simply with order but good order; with the welfare and happiness of the people; in short with commonalty itself. In this way the new science of police confronted the problem of the new order through a concept of coherence derived from the feudal orders. Today one would refer to the 'internal policy of the administration' rather than to the science of police, but this would obscure the important point that it was concerned with the substantial content of order as well as its formal preservation. The concept of police did not come into the world fully formalised, and the actual institutions of police were not fully organised in the state as a special branch of the division of labour acting upon civil society. In other words, 'police' emerged prior to the formal separation of violence from the methods and content of order. Even before its full formalisation it proliferated into a series of special branches: Medical Police; Lunacy Police, etc.

The range of the police conception is demonstrated in the sixteenth-century documents quoted by Knemeyer: 'Paragraph 29 of the 1521 *Reichsabschied* provides for regulations to deal with "extravagant clothing and consumption . . . blasphemy . . . monopolies, unseemly vendors, duties, weights and measures, and similar".'[32] Regulations that were brought to bear on the observance of contractual conditions show that the police concept played a central part in the establishment of private property and civil law. The strictly formal concept of policing emerged in the eighteenth century, but even then it still combined the meanings of commonalty and order. In fact as policing was broken away from the judiciary, the police concept increasingly referred to comfort and welfare. It was from the science of police that Adam Smith, for example, derived his political economy: 'Having now considered man as a member of a state, as a member of a family, and as man, we proceed to police, the second division of jurisprudence.' He defined police as civil policy in relation to the regulation of the inferior parts of government, which were: 'First, cleanliness and security; and second, cheapness and plenty.' Under this second head a specifically economic concept of comfort emerged as the production of wealth. Smith then introduced his famous discussion of the division of labour, which became the starting-point of the *Wealth of Nations*, and concluded: 'The establishment of commerce and manufacture . . . is the best police . . .'.[33]

This reveals the great part played by the science of police in the birth of classical political economy. And it also demonstrates that at the time this branch of knowledge took shape as a distinct science; order was still considered a unified concept encompassing the organisation of labour both inside and outside production. It pivoted on a single question which was never asked as such: how is labour constituted as wage labour, as distinct from any other form of labour? It was only when economics was established as an independent science that narrowed its attention to the production of wealth and the division of labour, that wider questions of sovereignty were hived off and dealt with separately under the head of jurisprudence. It is an illusion arising from the artificial development of economics as a separate discipline that the science of police only came into being to deal with problems of order outside production, and beyond the limits of the factory discipline.

The decisive event in the history of the British police was the formation of the New Police in the second quarter of the nineteenth century. In this period a conceptual break was effected between police in the formal sense, and what then came to be called *Social Police*. Social Police still continued to evoke the old idea of some all-encompassing order to be established by a great variety of measures, and in the early nineteenth century the idea of it attracted a broad alliance of intellectuals, reformers, merchants and bankers. It was the old science of police, expressed as a new administrative ethos appropriate to the triumph of liberalism, compounding traditional Anglican tutelage exercised over the rural labourer and Utilitarian impulses towards institutional rationalisation. Its proponents were inspired by colonial experiments in Ireland and India, where centralised power had been wielded with few inhibitions. In Ireland a modernised police force, Poor Law, and the lunatic asylum system were set up before similar developments on the mainland. In India a codified law of property was imposed on the village communes in an attempt to produce property owners and tenants. Hugh Seymour Tremenheere, first Inspector of Mines in the 1840s, was typical of the early inspectorate who subscribed to the administrative ethos of social police, and he was moved by an almost evangelical fervour for social amelioration. Although they had little statutory authority, their broad terms of reference allowed the new inspectors to press for improvements in the new industrial areas, which in the 1840s resembled the frontier towns of the United States at a slightly later date, more than the traditional market towns of Britain. Tremenheere wrote:

> The labouring population is with exceptions in favour of *some* land holders and a *few* master manufacturers, treated by their employers as mere brute instruments for the creation of wealth. To correct this – to bring the Christian principle of love for our fellow creatures into practical operation in favour of our ignorant and degraded drudges of the plough and the loom – appears to be the great task of the present and coming generations.[34]

The 1830s and 1840s saw the first establishment of the great bureaucratic structures of state administration to deal with poverty, disease, trade, insanity, etc. And once this had been achieved it was possible to eliminate the welfare and comfort elements from the police. This allowed the police to stand simply and formally for that department of state endowed with coercive powers. Conceptually this is the recognition that law is positive and derives from an existing political condition. The formal concept of police is therefore both the recognition and actual establishment of the order specific to industrial capitalism. At this point it became clear that the means (violence) to the social end (order) were contingent, and had to be organised in terms of that end. The police thus appeared as a pure or fluid force abstracted from society and arbitrarily set over against it; this being justified by the ends of law and order to be achieved. Only after the state had been theorised in terms of the freedom and the rights of the citizen was it possible to specify the object of police activity as the guarantee of the conditions of formal freedom.

The New Police was bureaucratically structured in such a way that it could bring to bear the appropriate amount of force exactly where it was needed in the shortest possible time. This tendency was consolidated by about 1870, and to move in that direction the New Police were freed from the political clutches of the mercantile gentry. Their predecessor, the Old Police, were too rooted in the specific social groupings of the previous century, and too deeply structured into the many overlapping jurisdictions to move fluidly across society. The Old Police were made up of a series of discrete entities, such as the Yeomanry drawn from the minor landed gentry and local vigilantes mobilised on the spot. By contrast, the new policeman belonged to a single body and took on the authority of the state simply by adopting the impersonal blue uniform and the appropriate mien. Control of the older structures had been in the hands of the Justices of the Peace, whose office was central to the power of the mercantile gentry. New stipendiary magistrates and reformed municipal authorities began to oversee police power. The New Police were thus one element in a wide-ranging project of bureaucratic centralisation essential to the regulation of labour in the liberal state, and not simply the result of some new search for order. Although there was no public demand for a new police, the problems presented by rapid urbanisation and industrialisation were mistaken for the dangers of a primary disorder in three fields:

(1) *Moral*: the possibility of intensive private action by volunteer bourgeois groups had been canvassed in relation to begging, drunkenness, prostitution, etc., resulting in Societies for the Suppression of Vice, Mendicity, etc. But the effect of these was nugatory, even when poverty had come to be seen as demoralisation, and working-class resistance in terms of wilful mobility and irregularity.

(2) *Political*: the concern here was with order on the streets, in open spaces and at the hustings. In the Gordon Riots of the 1790s, the crowd had taken over London with very little resistance, because the only effective instrument of order was the blunt one of the military. The ruling class were no longer willing to tolerate the food riots and rejected them as 'disorder'. Consequently the police became concerned with maintaining order on the streets.

(3) *Economic*: new large-scale productive and distributive insti-
    tutions, such as mills and dockyards, needed physical
    protection. Safer means of payment were developed.
    Smuggling, coining and wrecking were redefined as dangers to
    the stability of the market, and the appropriation of raw
    materials, which previously had formed part of subsistence, was
    cut down.

This apparent search for order, and the consideration of who
sought order, and over whom, does not provide the key to the rise of
the New Police, because it ignores the fact that the new order existed
prior to the working class, and produced it. It is characteristic of
modern society that its real order is intangible and appears only as
disorder which can always collapse into primal chaos. The advent of
the industrial proletariat in the nineteenth century, and particularly the large reserves of labour that flooded off the land, gave a
new urgency to this fundamental belief and further obscured the
order which was already fully in operation. The common view that
the New Police were developed to deal specifically with this
problem merely reinterprets history in the light of the illusion of
laissez-faire. What appeared as the seeds of primary chaos was in fact
the production of modern order, and the New Police were an
instrument developed out of this order to deal with the conditions
which it generated.

The most effective campaigner for the New Police, as he was for
the New Poor Law and health legislation, was Edwin Chadwick. In
1829 he wrote: 'Our present police consists of disjointed bodies of
men governed separately, under heterogenous regulations and
acting for the most part attendant on the earliest set of expedients
(i.e. violent punishment of infractions of personal security or of the
rights of property).' He found this totally inappropriate for the new
situation where labour had become extensively subdivided; the time
of the labourer more valuable than it had been; and where there was
great accumulation of capital. He campaigned for a 'preventive
police', which would anticipate disorder and damage to property:
'A preventive police then, or any police, can only be sustained in
complete action by complete information.'[35] This was an explicit if
incomplete recognition that an *a priori* order, i.e. one which is formal
in character, exists in modern society, and why force has to be
organised in a fluid fashion, applicable anywhere, at any time and
for any reason. This fluidity is guaranteed through the standard

protocols and logistics of operational procedures. These procedures are confirmed by case law, such as that which invariably defines accompanying the police to the station as a 'voluntary' act, despite the wishes of the individual involved. The legality of custody is loosely defined at law in terms of reasonableness, or the interests of justice. Police practice does not routinely violate due process, as this aspect of the rule of law has itself been evolved from policing procedure.

From a naturalistic standpoint where society is always on the brink of disintegration, the force exercised by the police to prevent the decay of the social fabric appears simply as pure force, i.e. force opposed to chaos. But since the 'disorders' of modern society arise from a highly developed formal order, the force that contains them is anything but pure, as the order it seeks to preserve is already structured into it. The fluidity of the force wielded by the police across the whole society, is the exact correlate of the universality of absolute property.

THE PRODUCTION OF PROCEDURES

The fluidity of the force which the police exercise over society derives from the organisation of its practices on procedural lines. But this basis originates beyond the police itself, for the development of procedure is in a very real sense the development of the state itself. Procedure is the most immediate manifestation of the order derived from abstraction. These standardised routines of modern society presuppose the unitary state ordering social classes: a special force confronting the general force of the proletariat. They can therefore be found in every area of state practice, nowhere more than in administration, where they have proliferated like a convolvulus around the body of society.

Modern administration arose in the gaps left by the ambiguities of property law and, in filling these gaps, created a new continuum of procedures in which the distinction between itself and law has been continually eroded. Today the traditional division of powers which separates the judicial from the executive function has become nominal. Administration is subject to law, but at the same time it makes law. In a parallel way the judiciary has administrative functions: Chancery practices in relation to wards of court were the origin of many present-day administrative structures, such as the mental health services and the education system. Administrative acts which create new law are embodied in statutory instruments, such as were used in the building of the canals and railways, and which became more widespread after the *Public Health Act* (1875).[36] Administrative law-making today commonly takes the form of a 'scheme', or delegated legislation, whereby local authorities are instructed to draw up a plan for, say, education, which has the force of law, and is submitted to the ministry for inspection. In this way an Act of Parliament empowers the minister to delegate the authority to make decisions which carry the force of law. A similar pattern is found in public corporations, service monopolies and nationalised industries. The Board of Agriculture (1889), the Board of Education (1899), and the Department of Scientific and Industrial Research (1906–14) offer prototypes of this practice.

Administration has been defined as the constitution in action: where constitutional law provides a static model of the state, administrative law offers a dynamic one. Formally, administration as a practice involving discretionary decisions, is contrasted to the common law, where decisions are claimed to derive from the application of fixed rules to specific cases. Administration therefore has a definite legal form, established in English law through High Court decisions early this century, which state that the administrator must not overtly act through precedent, so as to be seen to treat each case on its own merits. This bolsters the illusion of a neutral state consciously facing up to specific events and problems with an open mind. This is reinforced by the doctrine of subjectivity, which asserts in various Acts that the Minister has a mind, and that it is what this mind understands, or takes to be the case, that establishes the legality of an act; and not the traditional concept of rational behaviour used in common law. In other words, a minister's definition of a situation cannot be countered with the doctrine of what a reasonable man would have thought in his situation. These are the ways in which the executive is endowed with a mind, which appears absolutely blank. C. H. Sisson, a professional administrator and poet, claims that the official stands in an empty place in the constitution, and is comparable to a criminal, since his task is to operate procedures in a context of any or no ideals. In his image, civil servants have metaphysically empty faces like German generals.[37] But the mind of the executive is no more blank than the power of the state is force pure and simple. The state knows itself and its tasks through the category of order. It sees its own created order of private property as disorder, and constantly rehabilitates it in response to the developing contradictions deriving from the fragmentation of labour. One object constituted through this category of order is population, itself a category naturalising existing capacities and needs. By 1870 the wider law of labour was faced with the task of recognising the labour-power of the proletariat as a general force, but was no longer adequate to this task, and the gaps between legal forms had to be filled, in order to create a continuum of order. This process is administration, which addresses itself to particulars (does not have the immediate formal universality of law), and from these particulars creates schematised or partial objects, which although abstracted from the social matrix, leave traces of their concrete origins within the procedures of administration itself. Thus the law-and-administration continuum came into being, abolishing the specificity of both forms as they had been known up to the middle of the last century. This unity is recognised in practice in the specialty, administrative law. The law-and-administration continuum is founded in order, itself the state's apprehension of its task of maintaining private property as a universal form. The continuum is embodied in its procedures. Thus these are not empty, blank or technical. They are not techniques: great confusion has been caused, for instance, by Franz Neumann's characterisation of Nazi law as a set of technical rules aimed at efficient achievement of élite-determined ends.[38] Similarly, police procedures are not merely matters of technique, but set the nature of that force in society capable of confronting labour-power as a general force. They mediate the force of private property so that it appears as autonomous, pure and fluid; a special force adequate to its object: a social class. Once the police were established as a unified and fluid force, the state no longer had to distinguish between law and administration, and could proceed to reconstruct them as a unity.

The mass-produced procedures of administration have come to be embodied in social and institutional forms: the *office* as an urban social habitat, with its various means of reproducing, circulating and storing records; the *file* as an instrument of co-ordination and a record of official action taken; the *interview* as a new technique inserted somewhere between administrative discretion and judicial precedent. The requirement for personal enquiry built into much modern legislation gave rise to a new type of specialist administrator: the *social worker*.

Administration is law in the sense that it creates law, is subject to law, and acts through legal forms; and the law affecting administration (i.e. administrative law) is probably the greater part of all law today. The executive has certain directly judicial powers, but where such powers can be conveniently separated off from policy, departments of state frequently place them in the hands of quasi-judicial tribunals, of which there are well over 2,000 in Britain today, many of them supervised by the Council of Tribunals. These tribunals probably had their origins in courts-martial, and have proliferated ever since the founding period of the bureaucracy in the 1840s. Officially they are favoured as being cheap and informal, speedy and expert. Many of them are concerned with the conditions of labour, such as those established by the *Unemployment Assistance Act* (1934), and those established in relation to employment contracts. The public enquiry, by contrast, is usually reserved for matters involving land, such as planning, although there are also some land tribunals. The third 'factor of production', capital, has its own sector of the law-and-administration continuum: the corporation.

The public enquiry is a truly mysterious body: on the one hand it has to observe special procedures, concerns itself with policy, and is held in public: so that properly speaking it is not administrative. On the other hand, its decisions are not reached by applying rules and it enjoys wide discretion. So it would be equally wrong to characterise it as judicial. In short, the interpenetration of law and administration is so complex and the permutations of their mixture so varied, that the nature of the administrative devices in use today, and in fact the nature of the state itself, cannot begin to be grasped in formal constitutional terms.

Developments in the law-and-administration continuum which have taken it dramatically beyond the terrain of traditional constitutionalism can be seen in the quango, now an important area of policy-making. A curious confusion surrounds the acronym quango itself. In the USA it stands for *quasi non-government organisation*, where the conception is of government entering into contractual relations with private agencies, which are effectually brought into existence by the contract itself. Here we see an immediate conflation of law and administration into a single form. In Britain quango refers to *quasi autonomous national government organisation*, because it is conceived of in terms of its administrative link to the department of state which is its main client. Thus it is considered part of the executive, although not itself a government department. For this reason quangos are often referred to as fringe bodies.

Non-ministerial forms of democratic government were used extensively in Britain until the 1850s (e.g. the Poor Law Commission 1834–47), but then gave way to the ministerial department as part of the attempt to strengthen parliamentary institutions. From the first decade of this century boards and commissions, as the forerunners of quangos, gradually returned to use. Some simply bridge the gap between central and local administration, as in urban development. An example of the problems of founding municipal enterprise was the production of gas by the Manchester police authority in the early nineteenth century, in the absence of any other adequately constituted authority. Public corporations were locally established to produce gas, run transport, build harbours; and set up centrally to construct dockyards and arsenals. Vickers, the armaments producers, were virtually a creature of government from the 1890s onwards. In the interwar years public corporations were established to run the 'natural monopolies' of airways, electricity and radio. At the same time a whole host of boards were rationalising sectors of industry such as coal, cotton and sugar; simulating internal markets for milk, wheat, herrings and other fish; regulating imports, the currency, and the share market. After the war they provided finance for industry, and latterly the regulation of prices. Today fringe bodies are widely used in the fields of welfare, art, sport, and judicial decisions concerning licences and welfare payments. Professions, such as engineering, have been incorporated into the state by the same administrative device.

It is not only impossible to define these bodies in the traditional terms of juridical democracy, but they have become so all-pervasive that it is impossible to point to any area of civil society or private life that is not set in their context and structured by them. They represent the demise of civil society. The only thing that does seem clear about them is that they respond to the *bare imperative* of a particular situation, strain or anomaly in the social fabric: something simply has to be done. But having been done, official awareness of the process is dissolved into discussions of accountability and efficient management. The critique of quangos by Tory champions of freedom, being repeated by Social Democrats, is entirely disingenuous, since there are only two alternatives to them:

(1) increased ministerial power and the extension of the central civil service; or (2) the liquidation of the state itself.

The quango does throw light, in some instances ironically, on the emergence of the new law-and-administration continuum that has soaked up civil society in the desperate and doomed attempt to formalise labour. It is as if the state, reaching back into what it has already constituted, loses its nature as sovereignty, or pure arbitrary force, and in a way reveals its true nature as the force of private property. Through the categories or order and social class the law-and-administration continuum matches and touches the object it constitutes, population.

The legal control of administration is achieved through a range of means, characterised by their institutional distance from the bureaucracy. A series of semi-detached commissioners has been created to deal with complaints of maladministration, but these officials are compelled to separate form from content, and are not allowed to question the actual merits of decisions, only to consider the procedure by which they were reached.[39] The judicial surveillance of administration is founded on the so-called principles of natural justice, that no man shall be the judge in his own case (the administrator), and that no one shall be judged unheard (the *administré*). The only way the courts can intervene is by a series of medieval procedures, which aim to determine whether the administrative body under examination has jurisdiction in the case or not. Recent legal decisions have widened the concept of jurisdiction so far as to include virtually any legal error whatsoever.[40]

Administration cannot, therefore, be counterposed to law, since it is a particular form of law, officially the form of non-precedent, or discretion. Moreover, the distinction between the arbitrariness of administration and the precedent of the common law is itself unreal, since the courts are frequently arbitrary, as the examples of the Taff Vale case and *Rookes* v. *Barnard* illustrate. It is also unreal for the deeper theoretical reason that the force of the state, although it appears arbitrary and autonomous is, in fact, absolutely grounded in the order of property. Law and administration are now so closely compressed into each other that no meaningful distinction can be made between them. Various devices exist for subjecting law-making to considerations of policy, that is to administration. Administration itself, whether governmental or corporative, has been grasped as a unity even in official thought, through such concepts as management and administrative science. The continuity of this unified administrative process with the common law is expressed officially in the doctrines of administrative law. It is only in terms of their immanent and practical identity as a unified process that the state can now be grasped. Law, and now administration, are forms through which the subjects of social production are constituted by the state, but social production is in a continuous state of change and forms have to be recast in accordance with it. The subjectivity of formal equivalence is retained in the replicated procedures of the modern state and perpetuated by them.

POLICY

In the first half of the nineteenth century the political force that transformed the productive capacity of society into a commodity (labour-power) rested upon poverty as shortage. Even in the second half of the century, universal want could still be called upon to order labour, and the wider law of labour was formulated in terms of pauperism. Poverty as shortage was not invented in the nineteenth century, but put onto a new footing; and mobilised into a new productive force unparalleled in history – the modern proletariat.

The history of industrial capitalism divides into two phases according to the production of surplus value. The first, beginning with the industrial revolution and lasting a hundred years, was *absolute* surplus value. In this period real wages were held down and capital increased profits by extending the working day towards its natural limit. In the second phase, of *relative* surplus value, real wages rose, and capital turned to increased productivity and intensified labour to reduce the value of wage goods. In the closing decades of the eighteenth century, industrial capitalism emerged from the society of mercantile manufacture and began its historic struggle for domination over it; by the closing decades of the nineteenth century the outcome of this struggle was decided, and industrial capitalism was established on its own foundations. The keystone of the new order was the consolidation of the wage system and the completion of the labour market, where labour-power is bought and sold purely and simply as a commodity. These developments achieved stark maturity in the factories of the twentieth century, where new techniques of production consumed labour-power *en masse*. It was through these new techniques that the value of wage goods was reduced dramatically, and the standardised commodities of mass consumption made possible. The industrial revolution mechanised handicraft; the technology of mass production broke free from all earlier methods and organised the production of sophisticated products with unskilled and semi-skilled labour. In the process the machine was standardised as a product – the sewing machine, the car – and became an item of domestic consumption. This redefined the reproduction of labour-power, and decomposed the political economy of need into a subjective economy of want. In the phase of absolute surplus value the projection of labour-power onto the market, and the expenditure of the wage, were regulated by poverty (the market): by contrast the reproduction of labour-power for relative surplus value in the subsequent phase was effected through a dense matrix of controls (policy).

The emergence of industrial capitalism at the turn of the nineteenth century replaced simple with intensified property at the heart of the state; and since that time the development of the state has been determined by the laws through which labour-power is reproduced as a commodity. During the phase of absolute surplus value, modifications in mercantile law were sufficient. But the consolidation of the labour market after 1870 required a labour contract *sui generis* that could not be constructed through a simple extension of the common law to labour-power as private property. As a result the refinement of the narrow law of labour could only be effected through an elaboration of administration which impinged upon the wider law of labour and led to its reform. The theme of this reform, which took place upon a piecemeal basis over many decades, was social insurance. The abolition of pauperism as an administrative category was anticipated in legislation before the First World War; insurance was extended in the 1920s and 1930s; but it was not until after 1945 that the new wider law of labour was finally consolidated in the 'welfare state'. When the production of relative surplus value gained full momentum after the Second World War, social insurance coupled with affluence in the labour market to supersede poverty and shortage as the premise of labour-power.

The reproduction of labour-power is both formal and real. As a formal process it starts with the establishment of the population, and the crystallisation from it of legal subjects able to dispose of their own capacities as objects of property. Until late in the nineteenth century the subjectivity of labour-power was only loosely formulated through disparate legal elements – the *Master and Servant Acts* and fragments of common law. The real process of reproducing labour-power – the provision of means of subsistence – was equally labile. Direct allocations to the destitute through the Poor Law were sharply distinguished from the wage, but though this set workers and paupers apart formally, general shortage pressed a common stamp of misery on workhouse, factory and tenement.

The makeshift character of wage labour during the first two-thirds of the nineteenth century, and the exposition of the wider law of labour through the Poor Law, complemented each other. The improvised nature of these arrangements, whose elements were adjacent but not systematically connected, was the quintessence of absolute surplus value, where the momentum of accumulation came from individual enterprises and capital-in-general functioned only theoretically as an aggregate. By contrast the production of relative surplus value has systemic continuity, since the reduction in the value of wage goods upon which it depends lies beyond the scope of individual firms, and can only be effected by capital as a whole acting in unison. The increases in the level of real wages made possible by the fall in the value of wage goods, and the way this was achieved through the continuity of capitalist production – i.e. the real advent of capital-in-general – together determined the necessity for a reconstruction of labour-power, and the lines along which this reconstruction took place.

On the formal side, the first requirement was a more precise labour contract. To bring this about the subjectivity of labour was consolidated: into citizenship, through the extension of the franchise; and into collective right, through the legal recognition accorded to trades unions. On the real side, rising wages loosened the grip of scarcity as a means of ordering labour. The wider law of labour was reformulated, since it was no longer possible for the state to exercise the same leverage over the working class through the direct provision of means of subsistence at its margin. In the nineteenth century the workhouse was the perfect expression of hardship as the order of labour: it confronted the working class with its exclusion from both wealth and political right. The consolidation of relative surplus value in the twentieth century, by alleviating the pressures of hardship and refurbishing the subjectivity of labour, discredited it as a despotic anachronism. The introduction of social insurance in 1911 began the process of bringing the wider law of labour up to date.

In the nineteenth century the order of labour pivoted on

hardship; in the twentieth it rotates on the axis of consumption. All workers, those out of work as well as those who receive a wage, gain access to their conditions of life through money, whose orderly expenditure is vital for the stability of accumulation. Working-class expenditure always played its part in the circulation of capital and realised a significant fraction of surplus value. But the growth of real wages, and the emergence of whole branches of industry specialising in items of mass consumption, made the regulation of this expenditure a matter of urgency. In the nineteenth century it was sufficient for the law of labour to reinforce and formalise the pressures of scarcity that drove labour to the factory gates; in the twentieth century it has had more subtle tasks to perform:

(1) the determination of wages as a proportion of total value;
(2) the regulation of the wage as an element of the circulation of capital;
(3) the reproduction of the reserve army in terms that are consistent with the full development of universal subjectivity into citizenship; and
(4) the formalisation of abundance.

The reconstruction of the law of labour to achieve these ends was accomplished through a series of detailed acts which situated the working class inside the state. In the phase of absolute surplus value the working class was little more than a victim of property: in the phase of relative surplus value it became active in respect to both labour-power and consumption. This change was brought about through the state, but in the process the state changed and moved from reform to policy.

As a recent development which only gained impetus after the Second World War, policy contrasts sharply with social reform in the nineteenth century. Social reform built the legal and administrative body of the state to establish labour-power as the general commodity or force in society: policy set this body in motion. Its starting-point was the potential universality of labour; its purpose, to frustrate the realisation of this potential by incorporating the working class into the state and formalising class struggle. The period of reform was more or less over by 1870, but the structures of law, administration and finance that had been created by this time were inadequate for producing relative surplus value. Modifications were necessary: the franchise had to be made universal; trades unions permitted to exercise their legal rights; and the reserve army redefined in terms that were consistent with this new subjectivity of labour. It was these modifications of law and administration, together with the subtle requirements the new law of labour had to satisfy, that prepared the ground for policy and at the same time determined what this policy was to be.

The age of policy was symbolically inaugurated in 1944 by a government *White Paper* which carried a commitment to a 'high and stable level of employment'. Full employment was not simply one policy among many, but policy as such, since it provided a concrete synthesis of all its elements, conditions and requirements. It was only through full employment that the incorporation of the working class into the state and its active participation in the reproduction of labour-power could be sustained. It is plausible to represent full employment as the natural outcome of political developments following the age of reform; as the only possible corollary of the active subjectivity of labour; or even more narrowly as the only way in which social insurance could be set upon an actuarially sound basis. Certainly it would never have been established as policy without these developments; nevertheless it did not emerge spontaneously from them. It took conscious deliberation to bring into being, and a reconstruction of economic theory to demonstrate how its achievement and management could be made consistent with the intensified property relations of capitalist production. Numerous authors contributed to the new political economy in Britain – Beveridge, Macmillan and even Gaitskell: but one, J. M. Keynes, stood out, and his major work, *The General Theory of Employment, Interest and Money* (1936) takes pride of place as the prolegomena of policy.

The economic problem of the *General Theory*, the downward inflexibility of money wages in recession due to trades unions, and the solution it proposed, provide the classic theoretical statement of policy. In the 1920s, in a polemic against the return to the gold standard, Keynes had grasped 'the truth that we stand midway between two theories of economic society' with specific reference to the problem of wages. The theory he preferred was that 'wages should be fixed by reference to what is "fair" and "reasonable" as between classes'; the one he rejected was the 'economic Juggernaut' that 'crash[es] along . . . without attention . . . to individual groups'.[41] His objections to the 'Juggernaut' went beyond moral offence to a keen appreciation of the dangers it threatened. But if these dangers were to be avoided by offering economic security and prosperity to the working class, the problem remained of reconciling these concessions to accumulation and order. By the interwar period the grounds had been established for the active participation of the working class in the political economy of capitalism. The nineteenth-century law of labour had been extensively revised as the more positive subjectivity of labour had been established. The process of reforming the wider law of labour was well advanced, and the administrative definition of the reserve army as 'unemployed', which provided the immediate precondition for full employment, had been made. The tidal wave of struggles, which started before the war and culminated in the General Strike of 1926, underlined the permanence of trades unions as part of the political order, and the vapidity of the view prevailing among economists that they were simply market imperfections. The question was how could these developments be accommodated and how could capitalism be 'wisely managed'? The answer involved a recognition of the changes taking place in capitalism itself, in particular the intensification of property and a rejection of all prescriptions derived from the simple property-form. For Keynes this rejection took the form of a critique of neo-classical economics and the fetish of *laissez-faire*, misleading many of his readers, both left and right, as to the real nature of his project – the substitution of policy for politics.

The General Theory was a manual for policy written in the reified terms of economics, which obscure the relations of classes and the exercise of power. Keynes's views of the nature of the working class and its relation to the state were expressed as a theory of wages, and the implications of wage struggles for economic activity.

Keynes's theory of wages laid greater stress upon the wage as an element in the circulation of capital than traditional neo-classical theory, which took wages one-sidedly as a cost of production. This approach, of which Keynes was so critical, represented the economic theory of absolute surplus value. It took the individual capital as its standpoint and lacked any deep appreciation of capital-in-general, which figured as a simple aggregate. Since workers never spend more than a small fraction of their wages on the products of their employers, wages, for individual capitals, figure primarily as a cost of production. Neo-classical theory projected this position socially, and drew the conclusion which Keynes opposed so strongly: that the level of employment could be raised by lowering wages. Keynes's opposition to this conclusion rested on two grounds. First, it ignored the real difficulties of reducing wages, since it failed to acknowledge the significance of trades unions in the emerging economic order. Second, it placed much too little weight upon wages as an element in the circulation of capital (a component of aggregate demand) and could, in fact, be counter-productive by narrowing the market. Where the micro-economics of neo-classical theory represented the outlook of absolute surplus value, Keynes's macro-economics expressed the rising order of relative surplus value: it took capital-in-general as its standpoint, and recognised the active role of the working class in respect to both the selling of labour-power (trades unions) and the expenditure of the wage (the marginal propensity to consume). By treating labour-power as a commodity like any other in a market it believed to be self-regulating, neo-classical economics dimmed the light of reason and allowed the phantasmagoria of *laissez-faire* to flourish. By recognising the specificity of labour-power, particularly its new and active subjectivity within the context of social capital, Keynes simultaneously identified the central problematic of policy and the terms on which the state could assume authority. As the passive subjectivity of labour-power supported the doctrine of *laissez-faire* in the nineteenth century, its active subjectivity promoted the involvement of the state as the author of policy in the twentieth century.

By insisting that the active subjectivity of labour had become a fundamental fact of capitalist society, Keynes shattered the illusion of harmony, and replaced the social geometry of neo-classical theory with the hard politics of class struggle. But at the same time he moderated the shock by indicating ways in which working-class struggle could be domesticated. Developing his argument in terms of wages, which in itself takes the first and decisive step towards formalisation, Keynes claimed that the struggle over money wages 'affects the distribution of the aggregate real wage between different labour-groups and not its average amount per unit of employment [i.e. the value of labour-power] which depends . . . upon a different set of forces'. He continued: 'The effect of combination on the part of a group of workers is to protect their *relative* real wage. The general level of wages depends upon the other forces of the economic system.'[42] Trades unions could be tolerated, therefore, since their struggles were directed against individual capitals and other groups of workers, and not against capital-in-general. They could not exercise any direct effects upon the 'other forces of the economic system' which determined the social distribution of value between labour and capital. These 'forces', however, were not to be left to themselves, and much of the *General Theory* was devoted to ways in which they could be managed so as to regulate the distribution of value between labour and capital, and stabilise the level of employment. In this way Keynesianism (policy) proposed to reconcile the unreconcilable: within the political consensus of full employment it accommodated the freedom of working-class struggle and the sovereignty of the state in a way that appeared to supersede the traditional problems of capitalism. As the long post-war boom worked its economic miracles, this accommodation took on the appearance of a final solution, and it was only a few niggling conservatives who voiced doubts about the permanent viability of the régime of policy. The fashionable terms of the period – 'the affluent society', 'post-industrial society', 'the end of ideology' – express the ideal of policy, and the belief that it marked a decisive break with the past. The radical contribution to this illusion was the idea that the class struggle had become submerged into a wider international conflict between the developed and the under-developed worlds.

As a self-conscious synthesis of the politics of liberal democracy and the economics of public finance, policy produced a new fiscal demography – *national income* – within which politics was reduced to accountancy and social forms flattened onto a single plane. In the late 1930s Keynes showed a deep interest in the statistics of national income, and in *How to Pay for the War* (1940) pressed the need for official data as an instrument of economic management. The concept of national income underlay the *General Theory*, particularly the theory of aggregate demand, though it was not Keynes's invention. The origins of the national income concept in economic thought go back a long way. In an embryonic form it can be found in the writings of the physiocrats: Adam Smith's idea of the 'neat product' carried its development a step further. But its emergence in its modern form took place in the 1860s and 1870s alongside those other developments of the state that eventually resulted in policy. One of the earliest pieces of empirical research governed by the concept of a national income as such was made by Leone Levi in his *Wages and Earnings of the Working Classes* (1867). It was brought into the mainstream of economic theory by Alfred Marshall and given analytic prominence by A. C. Pigou, *The Economics of Welfare* (1920). 'Generally speaking', wrote Pigou, 'economic causes act upon the welfare of any country, not directly, but through the earning and spending of that objective counter-part of economic welfare which economists call the national dividend or national income.'[43] One of the first attempts at systematic measurement in Britain was made by Arthur Bowley and Josiah Stamp, *The National Income 1924* (1927), soon followed by Colin Clark, *National Income and Outlay* (1937). The first official estimate appeared in a White Paper in 1941: after the war the annual *Blue Books* of *National Income and Expenditure* became the most important compendia of political knowledge.

In constructing the concept of national income, the original authors ran into the difficulty that as the objective counterpart of welfare it should include all use-values, whereas economically it made sense to restrict it to exchange-values. In the end they opted for a pragmatic solution to the fundamental problem that wealth in capitalist society takes the form of commodities; they accepted the exchequer's fiscal definition of income in terms of money and based the concept on the modern mode of taxation. Subsequently the problem receded into the background and 'the *Blue Book*', as the Stones point out, 'does not waste any space on general explanations'.[44] As a result the political character of national income became buried in statistics, and it took its place alongside the other categories of order as an irreducible and self-evident thing-in-itself. Thus exactly the same questions are asked of national income as of population and money – what are its component elements and what causes it to grow? – while those pertaining to its nature are overlooked. National income is analysed in the same way as population and money because it is made up of them: historically and theoretically, national income is the *product* of population and money.

In the phase of primitive accumulation, wealth was piled up as value expressed in money as an object of property, and separated from its producers and consumers, who became subjects of property and took the shape of a population. Population and money are categories of private property and their separation from each other arose directly from this. As their product – literally, population multiplied by money income – national income overcame this separation, but the unity it forged was formal, not real. Thus the emergence of the national income category did not signify a new and direct relation of the needs and capacities of labour, but an intensification of the forces that held them apart. As one abstraction (money) multiplied by another (population), national income is abstraction raised to the power of two. It stands in the same relation to the intensified form of private property as population and money to the simple form. The latter were the fundamental categories through which political society crystallised out of the feudal orders, and with reference to which the state built the legal, administrative and financial structures of capitalist production. The former, national income, took over from this point. Placing wages and profits on adjacent lines and summing their totals, it already pre-supposes labour-power and capital as fully constituted equivalents, and establishes the terms in which law, administration and finance can be synthesised into policy. In the last analysis policy is the politics of distribution, and national income by compressing every section of society into a common monetary expression, is its perfect and indispensable statement. Historically it is no coincidence that the concept of national income emerged in the 1860s, at the time when the reconstruction of capitalism for the production of relative surplus value began; or that the official collection of national income statistics began in 1941, on the eve of the period of policy. For national income is both a product of modern capitalism and the concept through which it becomes conscious of itself. Both the theory of employment and the prescriptions of economic management (Keynes), rest upon the national income, which has superseded money and population as the fundamental category of order.

The theory of employment and its implementation as policy required the continuum of wages and profits be extended to the revenues and expenditures of the state, since variations in their balance contribute to aggregate demand and are decisive for economic management. Thus state and society were given a uniform definition as sectors (public and private), and the national income accounts, ignoring all qualitative differences, entered the transactions of state, labour and capital alongside each other. This continuum indicates the compression of the state and civil society into each other. National income accounting was therefore a product of the development underlying the generation of pro-cedures through which concrete events are subsumed into for-malised order. On the other hand, it is a procedure in itself; in fact, the *primus inter pares* of procedures, to which all others are finally related. It is the arbiter of procedure: first, because it is a procedure itself; and second because it expresses social reality more directly than any other. As the product of money and population it expresses

the productive capacities of society, and hence its real
determinations, in formal terms that can be recognised in the
rarified world of law and administration. The arbitration of
procedures in terms of national income defines the process of policy,
the terms within which it is formulated and implemented; but at the
same time it reveals its paradox. On the one hand the state is the
author of policy, with absolute sovereignty over its objects: on the
other hand, the procedures through which policy is articulated as a
process, by placing the state on a continuum with society, make it
itself one of these objects. In the age of reform the state kept its
distance, and its immunity from the movements of society allowed it
to build its institutions with relative coherence: in the period of
policy, the state became totally submerged in the blind forces of
social production and lost its head. In the 'concluding notes' of the
General Theory, Keynes proposed a union between the state, to
regulate the level of economic activity, and the free market, to
determine the allocation of resources, in which neither partner
interfered with the other. But the constitutionalism that underlay
this proposal had been reduced to an empty formalism by the very
developments which brought policy into being. Administrative
innovations before the First World War had narrowed the gap
between the state and civil society, and the implementation of
policy after 1945 closed off the remaining space between them. As a
result the reality of policy turned out to be the exact opposite of
what its authors intended and believed possible: instead of the state
bringing order to the instabilities of the economy, the movement
took place in the opposite direction. Coherent state-building gave
way to pathological growths, which created conditions as uncertain
as those that attended the transition from absolute to relative
surplus value earlier in the century.

Policy became the strategy for reproducing labour-power when
citizenship and the rights of organisation had been conceded to the
working class; and it was no longer possible for the state to cut
opposition off at source. Premised directly upon the class struggle
itself, the risk of policy is that it leaves the state with no solid ground
to fall back upon. Once it had embarked upon this course, and the
class struggle had been admitted directly into the political fabric,
the state had no alternative but to formalise struggles as they arose,
and shepherd them into appropriate channels. Contingent reasons
of consensual politics, and favourable conditions of accumulation,
buttressed this strategy after 1945, but its roots lay in the very

foundations of modern order, the nature of property, and in particular the special nature of labour-power. The threat to modern order comes from this special nature of labour-power as property, where subjectivity and objectivity are compressed together (the subject takes itself as object). This gives the possibility of the working class seizing both terms simultaneously in an act of revolutionary will. The room for policy is tightly circumscribed by this threat, and would not exist at all but for the formal distance between subjectivity and objectivity. By virtue of their universality the terms of private property are set apart: universal subjectivity is completely detached from all the physical conditions of life; while these same conditions, defined as objects of property, are totally indifferent to their subjects. This formal space provides the possibility for the labour contract to disregard subsistence. The separation of needs from capacities in this contract has in turn provided the practical basis for the splitting of working-class struggle, and made way for policy. Thus in relation to the labour contract the working class can fight as *subject-and-object*, as an alternative to fighting as *subject-as-object*: in other words, the terms on which labour is subsumed bring it into conflict with the forces of private property, but at the same time permit this opposition to remain within the political order. Policy exploits this possibility, and by conceding space to the working class to struggle as a *subject* of needs (for higher wages) *and* as an *object* of capacities (for control of the labour process), heads off more serious struggles that would unite needs and capacities in a struggle of *subjects-as-objects*.

Although the disruption of the potential unity of working-class struggle is a precondition for policy, it is no guarantee of its success over the long period, when the cumulative weight of even disorganised opposition exacts its toll. The formalisation of struggles-in-progress through policy has pre-empted revolution, but has forced on the state a mass of detailed innovations. Every movement of the working class that threatens to breach procedure has been countered with administrative initiatives – new boards, tribunals, statutory regulations, quangos. This pathological proliferation of state bodies indicates a failure of policy, which aimed not only to contain struggles-in-progress, but to minimise opposition with high wages and job security. In fact, the authors of policy placed greater emphasis on this preventive aspect of policy, believing full employment, supported by national insurance, would establish conditions of social peace. But, in so far as the success of policy hinged upon the ability of the state to maintain full employment and, at the same time, foster the orderly accumulation of capital, it depended upon capacities that the state did not possess. Although he carefully restricted his attention to the causes of short-period fluctuations in the level of economic activity, and set to one side the pace and pattern of accumulation that determine the level of employment through time, Keynes nevertheless embraced the view that the state could regulate the economy closely if only the personnel of government were prepared. He stated the aspirations of policy in modest terms of 'possible improvements in the technique of modern capitalism by the agency of collective action', but the implication of his analysis of money, is that he believed the state could draw the sting from the law of value. In the theory of policy, the sovereignty of the state is set alongside the freedom of social capital as a force capable of regulating accumulation; whereas this sovereignty is a condition of existence for the freedom of social capital. For this reason, coupled with the fact that there is no necessity for capital to accumulate in a way that offers employment to the whole of the available labour force, the brief given to policy was unrealistic.

The importance of full employment went far beyond governmental statements of intent, and its roots were planted deep in the state itself. Taken generally, full employment was the completion of liberal democracy, where absolute poverty and the compulsion to wage labour were construed positively as the right to work. Indeed, it was only when the objective necessity to labour was reconstructed into subjective right, that the availability of jobs became the issue of politics. At the same time, the redefinition of the reserve army of paupers into unemployed workers, whose situation in the labour market was of direct concern to the state, did not immediately follow from the broadening of the franchise. The link was provided by social insurance: by undertaking to pay money to those out of work the state placed the whole of the proletariat on a continuum, and shouldered an obligation it could not meet without regulating the labour market. Whatever other forces worked towards full employment, the fact remained that the only way the state could discharge its financial commitments to those out of work, without taxes on capital or public sector borrowing, was by reducing them to a minimum. The finance of relief through insurance contributions tied state liabilities to the level of employment, and set the conditions of policy long before it was theorised and became politically acceptable.

The legislation of 1911, although restricted to a narrow group of skilled workers, established insurance, but did not tie benefits so closely to the labour market as to precipitate policy. But the cynicism of one of the civil servants responsible for drafting the 1911 Act in saying that 'we had to consider whether we wanted the population to spend its time in bed or at the labour exchange', did not prevent the extension of cover in the following decades:

(1) An Act of 1916 covered a further 1.4 million workers and could have covered many more had it not met with passive resistance to contributions.

(2) The adoption under the Act of 1920 of what has been called 'universal insurance', although domestic servants and other groups were omitted.

(3) The adoption of the principle, if not the practice, of benefit as of right and in proportion to need with the uncovenanted and dependants' benefits in three Unemployment Acts (1921).

(4) The Blanesburgh revisions of 1927, which discarded the moral basis of national insurance by introducing the transitional benefit.

(5) The termination of all government control over the granting of benefit by the Act of 1930.

(6) The creation of the Unemployment Assistance Board in 1935, which established a government network of relief officers to supersede the local authorities. The Board had wide powers to give assistance indefinitely, according to need, to anyone regularly in insurable employment. It took over the relief of all workmen not receiving unemployment insurance.

These six measures retained employment as the founding category for reconstructing the wider law of labour in terms of social insurance, but they show the pressures of recession, and their originators were forced to blur the definition of employment and to relax the actuarial criteria as it became necessary to spread the net wide enough to catch anyone who could be employed. The modifications and extensions of the 1911 Act led to the creation of a vast centralised apparatus for the payment of a cash substitute for the wage to millions of men and women. This apparatus, the Unemployment Assistance Board, became responsible for the main body of relief after 1935, which though non-contributory, maintained the link with the labour market by making payments on a scale approximating local wage levels.

The Beveridge plan did not develop any new initiatives and, in fact, reverted to the original conception of unemployment insurance as the keystone of order. The developments of the 1920s and 1930s were more *ad hoc* responses to immediate contingencies than a systematic elaboration of the original Act. The major reforms after 1945, such as the *National Insurance Acts* (1946) and the *National Health Act* (operative from 1948), did not represent any major new departures in the state, and were little more than an attempt to consolidate on a systematic administrative basis developments started at the beginning of the century. This new welfare legislation retained the financial link established by the interwar measures between state obligations and conditions in the labour market, which then became the pivot of economic policy.

The development of social insurance played a decisive part in transposing the objective necessity to labour into a subjective right. In this respect it was crucial to the alteration of the terms on which the state met the working class – essential for the production of relative surplus value. But its novelty was restricted by the fact that relative surplus value is a mode of exploitation resting upon the reproduction of labour-power as a commodity. Thus the rights to subsistence it offered to labour were necessarily circumscribed by absolute poverty: had these rights crossed the threshold of formality and become substantial, ceasing to be rights and becoming conditions of life, the fundamental relation of capitalist production would have been severed, and the state would have put itself in jeopardy. The insurance principle avoided this danger by linking benefits directly to the wage (the contribution), but in doing so it inverted the historic relationship between wage labour and the reserve army. Historically it was through the administration of the surplus population that the state brought its force to bear upon the proletariat, and determined conditions for the population at work. Thus throughout the nineteenth century the narrow law of labour could be loosely formulated because the wider law of labour (the Poor Law) was so well articulated. With the advent of insurance, the state ceased to exercise leverage indirectly upon the main body of the working class by operating upon the residuum: in fact, it attempted to abolish the residuum formally as a category by paying it in the same way as the working population (money), and then making the magnitude of these payments directly dependent upon wages. With the introduction of policy after 1945, it went one step further and attempted to abolish the reserve army altogether by creating full employment. This would put insurance on an actuarially sound basis, and allow those out of work, for one reason or another, to receive generous benefits automatically. In this way the application of the insurance principle within conditions of full employment would transform the objective necessity to labour into a right to subsistence going beyond any political society had ever established – in fact far beyond the category of right itself. The political consensus of policy had a daring simplicity: the working class accepted wage labour unquestioningly, and in return the state undertook to provide universal wages by keeping the labour market buoyant and supporting the small minority out of work with benefits paid on conditions that did not impugn their integrity as subjects. Thus after 1945 the objective necessity to labour was buried beneath the streamlined principles of welfare – flat-rate contributions, equal benefits drawn automatically as of right, and universally free services. Liberal democracy, enhanced by the willingness of the working class to accept the conditions of wage labour, flowered into social democracy.

At the same time as the new order was promoted with an almost evangelical fervour as the solution to the problem of capitalist society within the framework of capitalist production, disguised as the mixed economy, the architects of welfare legislation saw the necessity to supplement insurance with a scheme of exchequer-financed gratuities. National Assistance or Supplementary Benefit as it became, was means-tested to keep the discipline of the Poor Law alive. National Assistance was never simply a safety net for exceptional cases: it was always the well-defined limit of social insurance, beyond which the objective necessity to labour could not be transformed into subjective right. The rules through which the welfare state regulated relief with respect to both insurance and supplementary benefit retained the rigours of the nineteenth-century wider law of labour as the basis for the new employment contract. These rules embodied the three conditions of wage labour: (1) *poverty*: the use of the means test stipulated exclusion from property as a condition of benefit, and gave the administrative board a power of discretion to determine needs that overrode the subjective right of the claimant; (2) *compulsion to work*: payments were only made on condition that the able-bodied sought work. 'The ultimate sanction is jail. It is a criminal offence to refuse to maintain oneself or one's dependants, and a handful of men usually spend a few weeks in jail each year for what amounts to a refusal to

work';[45] (3) *industrial discipline*: relief payments were made contingent upon comportment at work, e.g. rules defining industrial
misconduct. Grouped under these three headings, the rules on relief
replicate the three elements of contract: (1) poverty as desire to
consume; (2) compulsion to work as the will to enter exchange; and
(3) discipline as equivalence within the labour contract.

The numbers receiving relief through assistance were always
substantial and grew steadily throughout the post-war period (see
table 1). These limits to social insurance, however, do not detract
from its importance in transforming the definition of the reserve
army in the twentieth century, and changing the situation of the
working class within the state. But they do make clear: (1) in
general, that the objective necessity to labour can never be fully
transformed into subjective right within the framework of capitalist
production, where the capacity to labour is sold as a commodity;
and (2) that social insurance is only viable, financially and
politically, in conditions of full employment.

TABLE 1   *National assistance and supplementary benefit annual average
number of claimants, 1946–1981 (in thousands)*

1946–50	1,024
1951–55	1,704
1956–60	1,745
1961–65	2,012
1966–70	2,664
1971–75	2,895
1976–80	3,008
1981	3,264

SOURCE   *Annual Abstracts of Statistics*, (London: HMSO).

NOTE   These figures refer to claimants only; if dependants are
included the number living on supplementary benefits in 1979,
according to Tony Lynes, was 4,370,000.[46]

The collapse of anything approaching full employment in the
1970s is first of all a crisis of social insurance. Where the state secures
the conditions of labour-power directly through the labour market
with a well-defined employment contract, it is possible to alleviate
the stringencies of the wider law of labour and recast it in terms of
subjectivity. But when the level of employment drops, the wider law
of labour must take the strain of reproducing labour-power, and the
supplementary system of relief, supported by other agencies of

direct intervention, come to the fore. Thus the last few years has seen the growth of bodies operating on well-defined segments of the surplus population – for instance, the Careers Service as a body to manage the young. This development, together with initiatives at the other end of the scale, namely schemes for early retirement, give some clue to the future. In defining the conditions of life as objects of property and establishing a population of subjects, the state sets up the conditions for the growth of relative surplus population, and the way it administers this reserve army of labour sets the pattern for its activities throughout society. In the period of liberal democracy that began in the last third of the nineteenth century, a start was made to reorganise the reserve army on terms consistent with the production of relative surplus value. This led to the introduction of social insurance just before the First World War and its consolidation and extension in the interwar period. After 1945 policy carried these developments towards their conclusion, and through a commitment to full employment aspired to abolish the reserve army altogether. Now that the reserve army has reappeared on a substantial scale that shows no sign of reducing, the state is faced with a profound problem. A possible solution to its dilemma of retaining the crucial elements of social democracy in these conditions, would appear to lie in the political-administrative redefinition of full employment. In the period of policy employment has been measured in terms of those seeking work, and although the number unemployed has never included all those who would like a job, employment and unemployment tended to be general categories. There are already signs of this changing as the interpretation of figures of unemployment make special allowance for school-leavers. If this group were taken out of the labour market altogether, the retirement age brought down by five years; if housework were rewarded financially and the number of women seeking jobs were reduced; if the black inhabitants of the inner city were shunted on to the margins of the labour market through 'special aid'; the base against which unemployment is measured would be substantially reduced, and full employment would become a much easier target. Whether or not this approach is the one adopted, it would be compatible with the history of the state on the one hand, and with the forces at its disposal on the other.

The inability of the state to regulate the pace and pattern of accumulation to maintain full employment, *economic policy*, placed increasingly greater weight upon the formalisation of struggles-in-progress – *political administration*. The limits to both these aspects of policy is the state itself. With economic policy the capacity of the state to control accumulation runs up against the freedom of capital, which is its *raison d'être*: with political administration the limit is marked by the need for the state, first, to keep a tight rein on its expenditures so as not to impinge on this freedom; and second, to keep its institutions and their growth in order. As the emphasis of policy shifted towards political administration, this became increasingly difficult, since the development of the state no longer followed an order blueprinted by the specifications of intensified property (state-building). Initiative passed to the working class, and the state was forced to respond to movements it did not start. At the same time the working class failed to establish autonomy and has only been able to express its needs through the state: the result is the formalisation of these needs and frustration on the one side; incoherent growth amounting to pathology, on the other.

The premise of policy, which it must continually restore to guarantee its viability, is the corruption of working-class will into partial struggles for improvements within the order of abstraction. The formal possibility of this corruption originates in the fundamental structure of private property itself, where subjectivity and objectivity are established at so great a distance from each other as to provide grounds on which the working class can subdivide its struggles – i.e. struggle as subject-and-object as opposed to subject-as-object. However, this possibility does not realise itself spontaneously. On the one hand it needed space in the political order, which the state had to create by extending the franchise and granting legal immunities to trades unions. On the other hand, it required a willingness on the part of the working class to occupy this space, and, becoming 'indifferent to the final arrangement of things', place all its hopes in immediate improvements. The convergence of these positions into the consensus of policy after 1945 was anticipated by modernism at the end of the nineteenth century. Rejecting dialectics, modernists, on both left and right, embraced an empirical reason which affirmed the rationality of the liberal order by denying the validity of the grounds from which it could be criticised. Premised on the belief that a fresh substance could be fed into the forms of private property, politics ceased to be a struggle for ends and became a debate about means in which consciousness eclipsed will. The question of will, having been cut off from working-class politics, was dissipated by neo-romanticism, and entered politics through the medium of reaction (fascism).

Policy is a wedge driven into the class struggle: by conceding the rights of partial struggles it corrupts the will to struggle-in-general. But, by the same token, the class struggle is a wedge driven into the state, and the corruption of revolutionary will on the one side has the disruption of political coherence as its corollary on the other. Unable to seize direct control of its fate, for the last thirty years the working class has made history through the state and, in the process, pushed the state to its limits. So far this development has been grasped only by conservatism, which, with disingenuous naivety, diagnoses the state as the source of contemporary economic problems. But its politics of state policy are groundless. There is no possibility of reforming the state by means of the state, and regressing modern capitalism back to simpler forms of commodity production, while intensifying the production of relative surplus value. It is a reaction against the social democratic illusion that the forms of abstraction were empty and could be filled with a rational content.

THE SYSTEM OF STATES

To resolve the problem of capitalism and bring the law of value under control, economic policy is restricted by the freedom of capital which the state, by its very nature, is compelled to accept. To the authors of policy this limit to the state appeared extrinsic rather than intrinsic; a consequence of the national character of the state, and the absence of a world state corresponding to the global nature of capitalist production. Moreover this absence, and the instability of the system of states that stood in its place, appeared *sui generis*, and not the consequence of the state itself. In the period of state-building, when the working class was still under construction, this system of states with its diplomatic protocols and colonial facsimiles, was adequate for the consolidation of the political forms of intensified property. But once this period was over, the security of the state came to rest upon the formalisation of working-class opposition through policy.

In so far as they were not makeshift, the international bodies of the post-war period shared the premise of national policy, that the state is rational. In the eighteenth century a cosmopolitan constitution was imagined to supersede the system of states, determined by the same rationality that brought the state into being in the first place. This is implicit in Rousseau's contract, but Kant stated it:

> Just as universal violence and the resulting distress were finally bound to make a people decide that they should submit to the coercion of public laws . . . and found a state under a civil constitution, even so the distress of ceaseless warfare, in which states seek to subjugate each other, must eventually bring states under a *cosmopolitan constitution* even against their will.[47]

In the atmosphere of formal reason that prevails today, the logic of world order is expressed as a case for the advantages of stable exchange rates and liberalised trade relations: yet even so, the illusory rationality of the state remains the only possible basis for a wider policy. But no rational world order can use states as building blocks, since they are abstractions from rationality. The failure of international agencies is part and parcel of the failure of policy. The formality of diplomatic protocols expresses, as an external relation among states, the abstract nature of the order that rules within them. The absence of a world order is like the transplanting of Hobbes's state of nature to the political vacuum among nations, where private property runs riot.

Diplomacy, or the failure of the world state, is the natural habitat of the political state: the absence of the universal state expresses the formal, and hence imperfect, universality of the political state. In relation to a universal, everything is particular and derives its being from the process through which the universal constitutes itself. The world state would be a universal *par excellence*, and could only exist where nation states waived their claims to universality, and became particularities of it. But states cannot waive their universality, since they are not in full possession of it. Their universality is formal: the state can neither create nor perpetuate the conditions of its own existence. The real constitutive force of political society is social labour. This is the content of the universality of the state; so that any merger of sovereignties on a world scale would bring labour into a direct relationship with itself, and the world state would cease *ipso facto* to be political. The establishment of a world community through states contradicts the historical nature of the state as the antithesis of community.

At the same time the only possible basis for this community – free abundance resting upon the universal capacities of labour – already exists. But because these capacities have been developed through abstract forms, they exist negatively as the capability of mass destruction, and a vast relative surplus population (under-development). Weapons of mass destruction are the negative achievement of social labour: the possibility of social wealth formalised by the state into the capacity for global annihilation. The world state would, by that fact of its commonalty, inaugurate universal peace, free the capacity to create abundance, and lead political society to its dissolution. In contrast to the eighteenth-century dream of a world community constructed through a cosmopolitan union of states, it is clear that such a community can only come into being over the ruins of political society. Yet the absence of world authority to regulate money, trade, capital flows and so on, has dangers; since the irregularities of the world economy undermine the capacity of individual states to formalise opposition. The political state has two boundaries: an internal boundary where it meets social labour, and an external one where it meets a disorder of its own making. Under the pressure of the universal capacities of labour these boundaries are collapsing into each other, compressing the space within which the state moves, and threatening it with abundance on both sides.

Notes and References

CHAPTER 1: ABSOLUTE PROPERTY

Full bibliographical details of all works mentioned are given below (pp. 164–7).

1. These were the terms in which a legal doctrine known as the 'king's two bodies' was formulated towards the end of the sixteenth century. See Edmund Plowden, (1816) *Commentaries, or Reports*, pp. 213–50. This passage is cited in E. Kantorowicz, (1957) *The King's Two Bodies: A Study in Medieval Political Theology*.
2. Marx to Kugelmann (11 July 1868).

CHAPTER 2: THE THEORY OF THE STATE

1. J.-J. Rousseau, (1762) *The Social Contract*, ch. VI. Rousseau placed this passage in parenthesis – thus the use of the quotation marks.
2. Rousseau, *Social Contract*, ch. VI. The quotation marks are also used here for the same reason.
3. J.-J. Rousseau, (1755) *A Discourse on the Origin of Inequality*, part I.
4. Rousseau, *Social Contract*, ch. XI.
5. Rousseau, *Origin of Inequality*, part I.
6. Rousseau, *Origin of Inequality*, part I.
7. Rousseau, *Social Contract*, ch. III.
8. Rousseau, *Social Contract*, ch. VI.
9. G. W. F. Hegel, (1812–16) *Science of Logic*, ch. III, 'Doctrine of Essence – Actuality'.
10. G. W. F. Hegel, (1807) *The Phenomenology of Mind*, ch. VI, B.
11. G. W. F. Hegel, (1821) *Philosophy of Right*.
12. Hegel, *Phenomenology*, ch. V, C.
13. K. Marx, (1975) 'On the Jewish Question', in K. Marx and F. Engels, *Collected Works*, vol. 3.
14. K. Marx, (1973) *Grundrisse*.
15. D. Ricardo, (1969) *The Principles of Political Economy and Taxation*, ch. I, s. I.
16. A. Smith, (1776) *An Inquiry into the Nature and Causes of the Wealth of Nations*, bk I, ch. 5; cited by Ricardo, *Principles of Political Economy*, ch. I, s. I.
17. Ricardo's problem of reconciling the equal exchange of commodities with an average rate of profit, is one of the set pieces of economics. If production were achieved exclusively by living labour, as in the 'rude state', the exchange of commodities at rates proportionate to their values would accomplish the

equilibrium of distribution. When capital has accumulated an equal rate of profit must be included as an element of this equilibrium, but as Ricardo discovered, an inconsistency exists between this and the equal exchange of commodities. Ricardo explored the problem in detail in the *Principles of Political Economy*, ch. 1, s. IV, significantly titled: 'The principle that the quantity of labour bestowed on the production of commodities regulates their relative value considerably modified by the employment of machinery and other fixed and durable capital'.

18. K. Marx, (1969) *Theories of Surplus Value*, part 1, p. 367.
19. Marx, *Theories of Surplus Value*, part 1, p. 365.
20. Marx, *Theories of Surplus Value*, part 1, p. 366.
21. The attempts of the classical political economists to overcome this problem forms another set piece of economic theory. See Adam Smith, *Wealth of Nations*, bk 1, ch. 5; and Ricardo, *Principles of Political Economy*, ch. 1, s. VI. Political economy never made clear the distinction between money which is invariably the measure of value, and money as the invariable measure of value. In searching for an invariable measure it sought a counterpart for the natural equivalence of labour.
22. A. Smith, *Wealth of Nations*, bk 1, ch. 10; cited by Ricardo, *Principles of Political Economy*, ch. 1, s. II.
23. Ricardo, *Principles of Political Economy*, ch. 1, s. II.
24. 'There is certainly no general theory of the State to be found in Marxist classics: not just because their authors were for one reason or another unable to complete one, but because there can never be any such theory.' Nicos Poulantzas, (1978) *State, Power, Socialism*, p. 20.
25. K. Marx, (1977) *Critique of Hegel's 'Philosophy of Right'*, p. 32.
26. K. Marx, (1976) *Capital: A Critique of Political Economy*, ch. 1, s. 2, p. 132.
27. Marx, *Capital*, p. 92.
28. Marx, *Capital*, ch. 6, p. 272.
29. Marx, *Grundrisse*, p. 296.
30. Cited by G. Lukács, (1971) *History and Class Consciousness*, p. 95.
31. Lukács, *History and Class Consciousness*, p. 96.
32. Lukács, *History and Class Consciousness*, p. 98.
33. C. E. Schorske, (1955) *German Social Democracy 1905–17*.
34. E. Bernstein, (1961) *Evolutionary Socialism*, p. 13.
35. M. Foucault, (1979) *Power, Truth, Strategy*, p. 125.
36. E. Mach, (1915) *The Science of Mechanics*. See his *Space and Geometry in the Light of Physiological, Psychological and Physical Inquiry* (1906); and his 'Symmetry', in *Popular Scientific Lectures* (1910).
37. G. Bachelard, (1934) *Le nouvel esprit scientifique*, pp. 1–18, 71, 138. See his *L'Expérience de l'espace dans la physique contemporaine* (1937), and Einstein's introduction to M. Jammer, (1954) *Conceptions of Space*.
38. Bachelard, *Le nouvel esprit scientifique*, ch. 1.

CHAPTER 3: THE LAW OF LABOUR

1. Cited by J. Schumpeter, (1954) *History of Economic Analysis*, p. 251.
2. B. Mandeville, (1970) *The Fable of the Bees*, p. 294.

3. B. Pascal, (1670) *Pensées*, VII 'Qu'il est plus avantages . . .' pp. 51–60.
4. Cited by I. I. Rubin, (1979) *A History of Economic Thought*, p. 69.
5. D. V. Glass and D. E. C. Eversley (eds), (1965) *Population in History*, pp. 159–220.
6. N. Rose, (1979) 'The Psychological Complex: Mental Measurement and Social Administration', *Ideology and Consciousness*, pp. 5–68.
7. A. Milward, (1970) *The Economic Effects of the Two World Wars on Britain*.
8. It was found to be legal when a colonial High Commissioner suspended habeas corpus and imprisoned an inhabitant (see *R.* v. *Crewe; ex parte Skegome* [1910] 2 KB 576). When the state was shown to be guilty of serious illegalities it avoided the penalty through an Act of Indemnity (see *ex parte O'Brien* [1923] KB 61, A.C. 603). Acts of Parliament have recently given ministers the authority to modify the very statutes which empower them.
9. The most highly developed legal form is *persona* itself – legal subjectivity as such.
10. *Contract Re* was in fact confusingly known as Contract, but as indicated it did not resemble the modern law of contract. Slade's Case of 1602 highlighted the issue of whether there need be a specific promise in order to create an enforceable bargain.
11. Although Lord Mansfield's judgements were overthrown soon after they were made, they nevertheless represent the logical development of the elementary legal form of property.
12. Contract as legal exchange developed in relation to simple commodity circulation. But its significance is that commodity production became general only with wage-labour, so that contract is vital to any understanding of later capitalist production. In contract the separation of men from specific objects, so that they may relate as legal subjects to any object which embodies value, appears in feudal guise as a relation to a specific object *(persona-res)*; but its historical meaning is that the legal subject relates to objects that embody labour, or to his own capacity to labour, so that general subjectivity involves the subject taking itself as object.
13. The feudal corporation survived into the nineteenth century as a legitimate form of co-operative venture, but it existed directly within the state and implied central control and inspection. The sequence of events in the reform of company law is taken from: T. Hadden, (1977) *Company Law and Capitalism*.
14. A. Chandler, (1966) *Strategy and Structure*. This work discusses the emergence of a general staff in the corporation's central office.
15. Individual here means a particularised interest. From the early modern period this was often the household, within which women, children and servants were not full legal subjects.
16. Mercantile order did not take the form of standardised routines, which can only operate through liberal political forms. Mercantile arrangements existed in their own right, and were not inferior (partial, ineffective) forms of unitary state control.
17. Settlement was not an absolute barrier to labour mobility, and skilled workers did move and establish new settlement rights by the fact of being hired. The Old Poor Law, with its work-making and work-spreading schemes, and its system of undifferentiated rewards, enabled the larger rural employers to retain and dominate their stock of surplus unskilled and seasonal labour.

Settlement provided the model for colonial administration, with the authority of the District Commissioner being modelled on that of the JP. The attempt to maintain labour within the parish and only allow mobility against a definite offer of employment finds its modern counterpart in the South African pass laws and the Soviet labour registration system.

18. Magistrates did retain some powers over the poor under the New Poor Law, and were often included as one member of the new Boards. The centre of mercantile administration by the Justices of the Peace was the Quarterly Sessions, which fell into decay, although both the new police and lunacy legislation gave the magistrates new powers. For a different view, see: A. Brundage, (1978) *The Making of the New Poor Law 1832–39.*

19. 'The national government entered for the first time the life of the ordinary adult male able-bodied workman.' B. B. Gilbert, (1966) *The Evolution of National Insurance in Great Britain*, p. 287.

20. B. B. Gilbert, (1970) *British Social Policy, 1914–39*, pp. 284–300. The data for this period are perhaps extreme, but they do illustrate the important fact that for large sections of the working class the wage was insufficient.

21. Sir J. Collie, (1913) *Malingering and Feigned Sickness*, p. 15.

22. E. B. Pashukanis, (1978) *Law and Marxism*, ch. 5. The closest he comes to treating labour-power as a legal object is to note that immigration quotas have the effect of treating the proletarian freely seeking a market for his labour, like an object no different from other goods which cross national frontiers (pp. 112–13).

23. K. Renner, (1949) *The Institutions of Private Law and their Social Function*, ch. 2, s. II, I.

24. Sir O. Kahn-Freund, (1972) *Labour and the Law*, p. 8.

25. M. R. Freedland, (1976) *The Contract of Employment*, pp. 19–20.

26. A. Fox, (1974) *Beyond Contract.*

27. Freedland, *Contract of Employment*, p. 20.

28. 'The law had no share in advancing collective bargaining'; Kahn-Freund, *Labour and the Law*, p. 69. The standard reference work on legal history states: 'The state failed to control the formation and activities of these industrial associations'; Sir W. Holdsworth, (1965) *A History of English Law*, vol. xv, p. 82.

29. M. Tronti, (1976) 'Workers and Capital', *The Labour Process and Class Strategies.*

30. This judgement, by equating economic pressure in the form of the restriction of a flow of goods with physical violence itself, created a tort of intimidation without threats of violence as traditionally defined.

31. This suggestion is a perpetual theme of economic journalism.

32. F. L. Knemeyer, (1980) 'Polizei', *Economy and Society.*

33. A. Smith, (1964) *Lectures on Justice, Police, Revenue and Arms*, p. 155.

34. E. L. Edmonds and O. P. Edmonds, (1965) *I Was There: The Memoirs of Hugh Seymour Tremenheere*, p. 102.

35. E. Chadwick, (1829) 'Preventive Police', *London Review*, pp. 252–3.

36. In any given year the statutory instruments now dwarf the statute book itself.

37. 'It is the absolute nonentity of the British administrator that is his chief merit'; C. H. Sisson, (1956) *The Spirit of British Administration*, pp. 23 and 127.

38. F. Neumann, (1942) *Behemoth.*

39. These commissioners are known as Ombudsmen (meaning people's defenders)

and constitute one part of the administration of administration. The rest is made up of: committees of the legislature; royal commissions; the statutory audit.

40. A point argued in B. C. Gould, (1970) 'Anisminic and Jurisdictional Review', *Public Law*, pp. 358–71.
41. J. M. Keynes, (1933) *Essays in Persuasion*, pp. 261–2.
42. Keynes, *The General Theory*, p. 14.
43. A. C. Pigou, (1920) *The Economics of Welfare*, p. 30.
44. R. Stone and G. Stone, (1966) *National Income and Expenditure*, p. 7.
45. B. Stein, (1976) *Work and Welfare in Britain and the U.S.A.*, p. 30.
46. T. Lynes, (1981) *The Penguin Guide to Supplementary Benefits*, p. 26.
47. I. Kant, (1974) *On the Old Saw: That May be Right in Theory But It Won't Work in Practice*, p. 78.

List of Works Cited

Adorno, T., (1973) *Negative Dialectics* (London: Routledge & Kegan Paul).

Aristotle, *De Caelo*, bk. II, chs 2, 4.

Bachelard, G., (1934) *Le nouvel esprit scientifique* (Paris: Félix Alcan).

Bachelard, G., (1937) *L'Expérience de l'espace dans la physique contemporaine* (Paris: Félix Alcan)

Benjamin, W., (1979) *Reflections* (New York and London: Harvest/Harcourt Brace Jovanovich).

Bernstein, E., (1961) *Evolutionary Socialism* (1899) (New York: Schocken Books).

Beveridge, W., (1942) *Social Insurance and Allied Services*, Cd. 6404/5 (London: HMSO).

Beveridge, W. (1944) *Full Employment in a Free Society* (London: Allen & Unwin).

Bowley, A. L. and Stamp, J., (1927) *The National Income 1924* (Oxford University Press).

Brundage, A., (1978) *The Making of the New Poor Law 1932-39* (London: Hutchinson).

Chadwick, E., (1829) 'Preventive Police', *London Review*, February.

Chandler, A. (Jr), (1966) *Strategy and Structure* (Garden City: Doubleday).

Clark, C., (1937) *National Income and Outlay*, (London: Macmillan).

Clausewitz, C. von, (1832) *On War*.

Collie, Sir J., (1913) *Malingering and Feigned Sickness* (London: Edward Arnold).

Descartes, R., (1637) *Discourse on Method*.

Edmonds, E. L. and Edmonds, O. P., (1965) *I Was There: The Memoirs of Hugh Seymour Tremenheere* (London: Shakespeare Head Press).

Einstein, A., (1954) Introduction to Jammer, M., *Conceptions of Space* (Cambridge, Mass: Harvard University Press).

Foucault, M., (1979) *Power, Truth, Strategy* (Sydney: Feral Publications).

Fox, A., (1974) *Beyond Contract*, (London: Faber).

Freedland, M. R., (1976) *The Contract of Employment* (Oxford: Clarendon Press).

Gaitskell, H., (1939) *Money and Everyday Life* (London: Labour Book Service).

Gilbert, B. B., (1966) *The Evolution of National Insurance in Great Britain* (London: Joseph).

Gilbert, B. B., (1970) *British Social Policy, 1914-39* (London: Batsford).

Glass, D. V. and Eversley, D. E. C. (eds), (1965) *Population in History* (London: Edward Arnold).

Gould, B. C., (1970) 'Anisminic and Jurisdictional Review', *Public Law*.

Graunt, J., (1662) *Natural and Political Observations on the Bills of Mortality*.

Hadden, T., (1977) *Company Law and Capitalism* (London: Weidenfeld & Nicolson).

Hegel, G. W. F., (1807) *The Phenomenology of Mind*.

Hegel, G. W. F., (1812-16) *Science of Logic*.

Hegel, G. W. F., (1821) *Philosophy of Right.*

Hobbes, T., (1651) *Leviathan.*

Hobson, J. A., (1891) 'The Problem of the Unemployed', in Gibbins, H. de B., *Social Questions of To-day* (London: Methuen).

Hobson, J. A., (1922) *The Economics of Unemployment* (London: Allen & Unwin).

Holdsworth, Sir W., (1965) *A History of English Law*, vol. xv (London: Methuen).

Horkheimer, M., (1947) *Eclipse of Reason* (New York: Oxford University Press).

Jammer, M., (1954) *Conceptions of Space* (Cambridge, Mass: Harvard University Press).

Kahn-Freund, Sir O., (1972) *Labour and the Law* (London: Stevens).

Kant, I., (1974) *On the Old Saw: That May Be Right in Theory, But it Won't Work in Practice* (1793) (Philadelphia: University of Pennsylvania Press).

Kant, I., (1796) *The Metaphysic of Morals*, part 1, 'The Science of Right: Private Right'.

Kantorowicz, E., (1957) *The King's Two Bodies: A Study in Medieval Political Theology* (New Jersey: Princeton University Press).

Keynes, J. M., (1933) *Essays in Persuasion* (London: Macmillan).

Keynes, J. M., (1936) *The General Theory of Employment, Interest and Money* (London: Macmillan).

Keynes, J. M., (1940) *How to Pay for the War* (London: Macmillan).

King, Gregory (1695) *A scheme of the rates and duties granted to His Majesty upon Marriages, Births, and Burials, and upon Batchelors and Widowers, for the term of five years from May 1, 1695*, collected and digested by G. K. (London).

Knemeyer, F. L., (1980) 'Polizei', *Economy and Society*, 9, (2) May.

Korsch, K., (1966) *Marxism and Philosophy* (1923) (London: New Left Books).

Leibniz, G. W., (1717) *Correspondence with Clarke on God, the Soul, Space and Time* (London: James Knapton).

Lenin, V. I., (1909) *Materialism and Empirio-Criticism.*

Lenin, V. I., (1917) *State and Revolution.*

Levi, L., (1867) *Wages and Earnings of the Working Classes* (London).

Locke, J., (1690) 'An Essay Concerning the True Original Extent and End of Civil Government', *Two Treatises on Civil Government.*

Lukács, G., (1971) *History and Class Consciousness* (1922) (London: Merlin Press).

Lynes, T., (1981) *The Penguin Guide to Supplementary Benefits* (Harmondsworth: Penguin).

Mach, E., (1906) *Space and Geometry in the Light of Physiological, Psychological and Physical Inquiry* (Chicago: Open Court).

Mach, E., (1910) 'Symmetry', in *Popular Scientific Lectures* (Chicago: Open Court).

Mach, E., (1915) *The Science of Mechanics* (Chicago: Open Court).

Machiavelli, N., (1531) *The Discourses.*

Machiavelli, N., (1531) *The Prince.*

Macmillan, H., (1933) *Reconstruction: A Plea for a National Policy* (London: Macmillan).

Macmillan, H., (1938) *The Middle Way* (London: Macmillan).

Maier, C. S., (1975) *Recasting Bourgeois Europe* (New Jersey: Princeton University Press).

Malthus, R., (1798) *An Essay on the Principle of Population.*

Mandeville, B., (1970) *The Fable of the Bees* (1714) (Harmondsworth: Penguin).

Marshall, A., (1961) *Principles of Economics* (London: Macmillan).

Marx, K., (1969) *Theories of Surplus Value* (London: Lawrence & Wishart).

Marx, K., (1971) *A Contribution to the Critique of Political Economy* (1859) (London: Lawrence & Wishart).

Marx, K., (1973) *Grundrisse* (1857/8) (Harmondsworth: Penguin, in association with New Left Review).

Marx, K., (1975) 'On the Jewish Question' (1843), in Marx, K. and Engels, F., *Collected Works*, vol. 3 (London: Lawrence & Wishart).

Marx, K., (1976) *Capital: A Critique of Political Economy* (1867) (Harmondsworth: Penguin, in association with New Left Review).

Marx, K., (1977) *Critique of Hegel's 'Philosophy of Right'* (1843) (Cambridge University Press).

Marx, K. and Engels, F., (1848) *The Communist Manifesto*.

Marx, K. and Engels, F., (1934) *Selected Correspondence* (1846–95) (London: Lawrence & Wishart).

Milward, A., (1970) *The Economic Effects of the Two World Wars on Britain* (London: Macmillan).

Neumann, F., (1942) *Behemoth* (London: Victor Gollancz).

Newton, I., (1687) *Principia Mathematica*.

Pascal, B., (1670) *Pensées* (Paris: G. Desprez).

Pashukanis, E. B., (1978) *Law and Marxism* (London: Ink Links).

Petty, Sir W., (1686) *Essay Concerning the Multiplication of Mankind*.

Petty, Sir W., (1690) *Political Arithmetick*.

Petyt, W., (1680) *The Antient Right of the Commons of England asserted*, and *Miscellanea Parliamentaria* (London).

Pigou, A. C., (1920) *The Economics of Welfare* (London: Macmillan).

Plowden, E., (1816) *The Commentaries, or Reports* (London: S. Brooke).

Poulantzas, N., (1978) *State, Power, Socialism* (London: New Left Books).

Raphael, M., (1968) *The Demands of Art* (London, Routledge & Kegan Paul).

Renner, K., (1949) *The Institutions of Private Law and their Social Function* (London: Routledge & Kegan Paul).

Ricardo, D., (1969) *The Principles of Political Economy and Taxation* (1817) (London: J. M. Dent).

Rosdolsky, R., (1977) *The Making of Marx's 'Capital'* (London: Pluto Press).

Rose, N., (1979) 'The Psychological Complex: Mental Measurement and Social Administration', *Ideology and Consciousness*, 5, Spring, pp. 5–68.

Rousseau, J.-J. (1755) *A Discourse on the Origin of Inequality*.

Rousseau, J.-J. (1762) *The Social Contract*.

Rubin, I. I., (1979) *A History of Economic Thought* (1929) (London: Ink Links).

Schorske, C. E., (1955) *German Social Democracy 1905–1917* (New York: John Wiley).

Schumpeter, J., (1954) *History of Economic Analysis* (London: Allen & Unwin).

Sisson, C. H., (1956) *The Spirit of British Administration* (London: Faber).

Smith, A., (1776) *An Inquiry into the Nature and Causes of the Wealth of Nations*.

Smith, A., (1964) *Lectures on Justice, Police, Revenue and Arms* (New York: A. M. Kelley).

Stein, B., (1976) *Work and Welfare in Britain and the U.S.A.* (London: Macmillan).

Stephen, Sir S. F., (1967) *Liberty, Equality, Fraternity* (1873) (Cambridge University Press).

Stone, R. and Stone, G., (1966) *National Income and Expenditure* (London: Bowes & Bowes).

Tronti, M., (1976) 'Workers and Capital', *The Labour Process and Class Strategies*, CSE Pamphlet no. 1 (London: Stage 1).

Weber, M., (1964) *The Theory of Social and Economic Organisation* (London: Collier-Macmillan).

Index

Index

Index

3# Index

3# Index

Index

Mach, Ernst 75
Machiavelli, N.   26, 36, 67–9
Macmillan, H.   141
Making of Marx's 'Capital'   66
Malingering   110
Malthus, R.   85–7, 105
Mandeville, Bernard   87
Mansfield, Lord   99, 100, 118
Marshall, Alfred   108, 144
Marx, K.   12, 13, 17, 24, 28, 34, 39, 44–67, 69–72, 76, 77, 79, 93, 104
Marxism and Philosophy   66
Mass production   138
Master and Servant Act (1875)   116, 139
Master of the Offices   97
Materialism and Empirio-Criticism   75
Melancholy   12
Mental Health Act   95
Mill, J. S.   41
Mind   43
Ministry of Munitions   94
Modern property   3, 4
Modern society   23, 64, 66, 81, 82, 84, 93, 100, 112
Modernism   26, 64, 65, 72–4
Monarch
  personal capacity of   13
  two-body doctrine   12–15, 19
Monetary system   55, 90
Money   6, 145, 146
Mortality tables   88, 89

National Assistance   152
National Health Act   151
National Health Insurance   110
National income   144–7
National Income 1924   145
National Income and Outlay   145
National insurance   148, 150
National Insurance Act (1911)   108–10
National Insurance Act (1946)   151
Natural law   6, 19, 23–5, 27, 30, 32, 38, 42, 44, 47, 52, 79
  philosophy of   13
  route taken   3
  value in   53
Natural powers, death and destruction of   36
Natural property   84

Needs and capacities   1
Negligence   109
Neumann, Franz   133
Newton, I.   24, 75–7, 80
Newtonian logic   40

On War   68
Order   81–93
Outdoor relief   104, 105

Parallel machinery   117
Parties to the contract   119
Pascal, Blaise   88, 92
Pashukanis, E. B.   111
Pauperism   104, 138
Penal confinement   90
Perpetuities   101
Persona-res   2, 4, 8, 9, 97, 100
Petty, Sir William   87, 89
Petyt, W.   87
Phenomenology of Mind   40, 45
Philosophy of natural law   13
Philosophy of Right   38–46
Picketing case law   117, 122
Pigou, A. C.   108, 144
Pluralism   37
Police   111, 123–31
Policy   137–56
Political administration   155
Political economy   7, 46, 49–51, 53, 58, 59, 70, 76, 127
Political philosophy   7, 22, 26, 46, 58, 63, 67, 93
Political society   7, 24, 25, 27–32, 47–9, 51, 52, 59, 61, 63, 69, 79, 84, 93, 124, 158
Political strategy   68
Political theory   24, 26, 74
Politics and nature   15–16, 19
Poor Law   103–9, 115, 125, 128, 139, 151, 152
Poor Law Amendment Act (1834)   101, 104–6
Poor Law Commission   106
Population   81–93, 145, 146
  as fully developed category   91
  as uniform category of administration   91
  concept of   90